Godfrey Harris

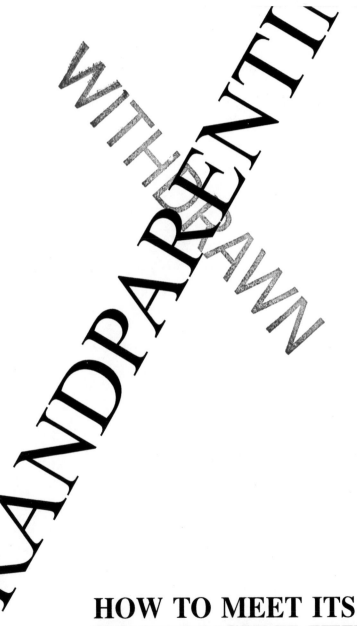

GRANDPARENTI

**HOW TO MEET ITS
RESPONSIBILITIES**

$16.95

GRANDPARENTING

How to Meet Its Responsibilities

Godfrey Harris

THE AMERICAS GROUP
9200 Sunset Blvd., Suite 404
Los Angeles, CA 90069 USA

FIRST EDITION
1st Printing—September 2002

The Americas Group
9200 Sunset Blvd., Suite 404
Los Angeles, California 90069-3506
U.S.A.

☎   + (1) 310 278 8038
FX   + (1) 310 271 3649
EM   hrmg@aol.com
WWW   AMERICASGROUP.COM

ISBN:
0-935047-38-7

Library of Congress Catloging-in-Publication Data

(pending)

Printed in the United States of America by
Fidlar Doubleday, Kalamazoo, Michigan 49009

TABLE OF CONTENTS

DEDICATION

To our grandchildren—Kevin, Alexandra, Scott, Sammy, Maya, and Devin—whose participation in the future provided part of the impetus to consider some of the themes presented in the pages that follow.

OTHER BOOKS BY GODFREY HARRIS

The Essential Travel Planning Kit
The Essential Event Planning Kit—1st, 2nd, & 3rd Editions
Watch It!
Concentration—1st & 2nd Editions (with Kennith L Harris)
Let Your Fingers Do the Talking
Talk Is Easy
The Ultimate Black Book—3rd Edition
  (with Kennith L Harris & Mark B Harris)
Don't Take Our Word for It
How to Generate Word of Mouth Advertising
  (with Gregrey J Harris)
Promoting International Tourism—
  1st & 2nd Editions (with Kenneth M. Katz)
European Union Almanac—1st & 2nd Editions
  (with Hans J. Groll & Adelheid Hasenknopf)
The Panamanian Problem (with Guillermo de St. Malo A.)
Mapping Russia and Its Neighbors (with Sergei A. Diakonov)
Power Buying (with Gregrey J Harris)
Talk Is Cheap (with Gregrey J Harris)
The Fascination of Ivory
Invasion (with David S. Behar)
The Ultimate Black Book—2nd Edition (with Kennith L Harris)
The Ultimate Black Book—1st Edition
The Panamanian Perspective
Commercial Translations (with Charles Sonabend)
From Trash to Treasure (with Barbara DeKovner-Mayer)
Panama's Position
The Quest for Foreign Affairs Officers (with Francis Fielder)
The History of Sandy Hook, New Jersey
Outline of Social Sciences
Outline of Western Civilization

FOREWORD

Grandparents are among the most valuable and least utilized resources available to Western societies. As a lifelong student, occasional teacher, published author, and involved activist in politics around the world, I have come to the conclusion that many communities would be better places to live and could provide greater opportunities for everyone if *grandparents* were more directly engaged in specific aspects of the upbringing of their grandchildren.

This book explores the topic of how grandparents can become more substantively involved with their grandchildren without interfering in the traditional interaction between parents and kids. It looks at the subject from the perspective of a public policy specialist, someone professionally interested in creating better communities through political activity. It leaves to other professionals—doctors, psychologists, teachers, counselors, mentors, ministers, and the like—the issues of how to make better kids for those communities. Some grandparents will be disappointed to learn, now that their children are grown, that someone thinks they have new obligations to future generations; some parents will be appalled to hear that *their* parents are being encouraged to assume any role in the upbringing of *their* kids. Both of these groups are not likely to get beyond this page. That's a shame.

As for the rest of you who will read on, I can only applaud your open mind and curious spirit. I hope the journey through these pages will prove to be worth your while and that the ideas offered will serve you, your family, and your neighbors well in the future.

Godfrey Harris

Los Angeles, California
September 2002

INTRODUCTION

INTRODUCTION

This book is about the *responsibilities* of grandparenting. We see the need to meet these responsibilities whenever grandparents are with their grandchildren—on their own or in the presence of their parents.

The very idea that grandparents have any *responsibilities* will come as a shock to many. These people believe that they and others have arrived at the status of grandparenthood with no duties to fulfill. They are the ones who smile when they see infants wearing T-shirts with legends such as "That's It! I'm going to Grandma's" or see a cartoon showing a little kid emerging from a sports stadium loaded with souvenirs, saying "What I like most about you, Grandpa, is that you don't give 'no' for an answer." ^^

---

^ The sources for statements in quotation marks can be found under the appropriate page number in the Bibliographical Notes section. A carat mark— ^— indicates that an additional comment or further information on the point can also be found there.

These grandparents seem to see their role in the same way countless others have seen it before them:

Provide grandchildren with undivided attention mixed with unlimited love. Worry only about such matters as whether they will call you Nanna or Granny, Grandpa or Gramps.

It is, as so many grandparents will tell you, a recipe for enjoying the thrill of watching grandchildren grow toward and into adulthood without having to be concerned about the issues and decisions that come at every stage of a child's maturation.

Most grandparents we have met—and those of qualifying circumstances that haven't quite gotten there—would agree that their own grown kids generally like this kind of arrangement. The adult kids want to raise *their* kids *their* way, following ideas they will have developed over the years, not necessarily as they themselves were brought up. This holds whether or not they think their own parents did a superior job raising them.

Some realize that their parents didn't always have the right answers about life and happiness, given the number who got divorced, moved from place to place, worried about how to earn or save enough money to live on, struggled to stay up with the Joneses, or failed to pay a lot of attention to what their kids were doing.

As a real estate agent living in Greenwich, Connecticut, commented upon learning that Bobby Kennedy's nephew, Michael Skakel, had been convicted of murdering a neighbor more than 25 years before: "The difference between '70s and '90s parents is that people now are overly everything with their children—overly indulgent, overly concerned, overly worried about achievement. But at least *they're* watching."

Further, most new Mommies and Daddies were themselves brought up by parents who did not have the information resources now available through websites and Internet chat lines.^ Some of them even think about the suffering their parents must have experienced making do without a library of videotapes or a stack of DVDs to keep the kiddies occupied before television was commonplace or when it became unavailable, unsuitable, or boring.

Even more of a disconnect is the fact that many mothers of the last generation probably stayed at home during the years their kids were in elementary or middle school and only the fathers worked out of the house. Come to think of it, did they have microwave ovens back then? Calculators? Cell phones? VCRs? Faxes? Was Baby Gap or Pottery Barn Kids around? How about SUVs? Did they know about DNA or Amazon.com or even car seats? Could you get seedless watermelons in those days or have hot pizza delivered to the house?

No doubt it was a different world. Moreover, consulting parents about raising their new grandchildren creates its own problems. One set of parents would surely have one idea about how to work through a baby's crying fit; the other parents might disagree.^ If you have any doubt about how differently the world can look to the parents of either the husband or wife, watch an episode of the television series *Everybody Loves Raymond* when the in-laws are in play. It suggests that new parents know they can't win in these situations; somebody will be offended when his or her advice is ignored. So why bother soliciting that advice in the first place?

There is another perceived reason to raise kids without grandparent involvement. As most newly minted parents see it today, they followed their parents' rules without any input into how those rules were written or enforced. Now it's their turn to set what they probably think are more rational rules for their own kids. And they can do so by taking advantage of the latest research, interesting ideas, and most recent opinion surveys. It's easy when you can EMail other new parents, read material available only on-line, listen to a string of radio psychologists offering valuable opinions, or glance at any one of a dozen magazines to learn what experts think as well as how celebrities and fashionistas are raising *their* kids.

Every new grandparent has observed all of this. They accept the fact that their kids want a chance to do it their way. They say, "Fine. Do it!"^

But some grandparents refuse to make the leap from this point to an acceptance of the companion dictum that therefore they have *no* substantive role to play in how their grandchildren deal with the world around them.

I am among them. My wife and I currently have six grandchildren between us.

I believe very strongly that I, as a grandparent, have an *obligation* to involve myself in the lives of our grandchildren in one specific way—how they react to others and

to circumstances around them in a public setting!

I fully realize that some of what I write may not be fully appreciated by all of our kids; past experience suggests that many of the ideas will simply disappear in a black hole never to be mentioned again. My wife and I have also noticed that some of our kids get uneasy when the focus shifts from the little ones to the older ones in the family. That's all right, too.

But having said all of this, I also accept that expressing myself about the grandchildren is just one more thing that comes with the territory of grandparenting. I am not trying to win votes in a family debate or get the parents to agree with my point of view, although I hope they will. In the end, though, I am simply trying to make a better world for myself and others in a way that makes sense to me.

Some grandparents, of course, may reject these ideas as too dangerous to their relationship with their own kids. Completely understandable. No one can expect 100% agreement and no one wants his kids to be apprehensive about what he does around his grandchildren. I hope only that those exposed to the ideas presented here will give them some thought and discuss them within the family. Whatever happens, we hope grandparents get a chance at imbedding something of themselves and their beliefs in community in their grandchildren.

Now if your kids gave you this book as a gift, it may be an invitation to start thinking differently about your responsibilities toward the grandchildren. If your kids spotted it at the side of your bed or on a coffee table, you may want to offer to lend it to them when you are finished.

Finally, if you have examples to reinforce the points made here or if you don't agree with some of the ideas we express, please feel free to contact the author in care of the publisher. We would love to include your thoughts and comments—with your permission and appropriate credit, of course—in subsequent editions.

BASIC CONCEPT

BASIC CONCEPT

Here, then, is the essence of my belief.

Grandparents, by virtue of what they have seen and done throughout their lives, represent an important community resource. I believe that if grandparents assume greater responsibility toward their grandchildren in specific ways, our society will be better for it.

I also believe that the responsibilities of grandparents toward their grandchildren are totally separate from the responsibilities that parents bear to the same children. While the burden parents carry is without question much heavier, the responsibilities of grandparents are no less important. As a result, I believe that both forms of responsibility can exist side by side without interfering with each other.

Here is another way to look at the parent/grandparent equation: Parents have to teach children how to deal with the world around them as they find it; grandparents can enrich the outlook and widen the point of view for their grandchildren. Think of parents as the *text,* grandparents as *supplemental reading.* As I see it, the primary interest of parents is to make better *children*; the primary interest of grandparents is to make better *communities* with the help of those children.

These statements on the responsibilities of grandparents clearly suggest that I believe the role involves much more than simply buying grandchildren frequent gifts, providing them with a stream of outings, serving them as taxi drivers, offering them custodial care, or acting as their banker of last resort. In my view, grandparents must also do a lot more than merely repeat stories to prove how clever their grandkids are, carry photographs to show how beautiful they are, or remember birthdays with a cascade of presents to show how deserving they are.

Never forget that batteries die, strings fray, plastic cracks, balls leak, metal rusts, parts weaken, pieces disappear, springs break; the lessons of life that grandparents can offer last forever. But note this, too: The responsibilities of grandparenting advocated here do not *exclude* anything else a grandparent might want to do for his or her grand-children. Love them, respect them, indulge them all you want. Give them all the attention they need.^ Be supportive of their activities and proud of their accomplishments. Just don't forget that there are those of us who believe you have a duty to help them understand what constitutes a better community for all.

At its essence, then, this discussion is about how grandparents can impart their thoughts on a better community. This is not by any means an exclusive undertaking; parents will offer their own thoughts to the kids as well. But it is designed to help anyone fill in the gaps should they appear and appreciate the more substantive aspects of grandparenting.

The role is basically *societal* in nature. Grandparents have a responsibility to show their grandchildren how they would like them to react to situations in public in order to help make a better community for all and to help preserve the civilization.^^

To make all of this clear, perhaps it would be best to indicate at the outset what this book does *not*

---

^ See footnote on p. 12 for an explanation of carat mark.

deal with. For one thing, this book does not discuss how to *raise* grandchildren—whether as observers, as day-care surrogates, or as full-time substitute parents; that is something we leave to others. Further, this book is not about the basic values or individual attitudes that kids should be exposed to; that is something we leave to parents and teachers, ministers and doctors, counselors and mentors, and the grandparents themselves. Instead, this book is about...

...how children should be exposed to what is expected of them in interactions with others of all ages and in all social situations.

Is it such a radical idea to ask grandparents to fulfill a primary responsibility of ensuring that their grandchildren understand how to deal with conditions *outside* of the cocoon of home, school, and church? We don't think so. Grandparents, by virtue of their greater age and differing life experiences, have a perspective that no parent can duplicate. After all, grandparents have a place in the community equal to that occupied by anyone else of any age or status. And being grandparents certainly does not disqualify them from having feelings or desires or acting on their beliefs when they are moved to do so.

Grandparents are entitled to want to see their community evolve in a direction and at a pace that are comfortable for them as much as anyone else living there. They have a right to expect people with whom they come into contact—children and adults alike!—to act in a way that keeps the grandparents comfortable.

In articulating a *primary* role for grandparents in helping their grandchildren to understand and operate in the larger society, we are not suggesting that this is exclusively their province alone. The parents need not be mute about how *they* want the community to function. They ought to share any views they have with their children and their parents as well. But with so much going on in so many lives today, some things get missed. If grandparents accept their responsibility, society will not have lost an important element of its continuing stability.

While it is always difficult, and sometimes dangerous, to deal with what strangers do in public, it is not something that anyone need be nervous about with his or her own grandchildren. On the contrary, if all grandparents were to impart basic societal values to their grandchildren, grandparents might not have to deal as much with the questionable public behavior of strangers. Take the following true story that happened to me a short while ago.

I was with a client at his store. In the middle of our discussion, I realized that I had forgotten something in my car. On the way to retrieving it, I noticed two young men watching me. As I approached the car, one spit hard; then the other followed suit. It was clear that the expectorations were aimed to land directly in front of me. I was infuriated at the insult. Worse, I was still battling the effects of an exotic virus that had kept me out of my office for four months and concerned with the potential danger of some new disease assaulting my weakened immune system.

As I revved up my mind and warmed up my tongue to give these two teenagers an example of how angry someone can get when provoked, I heard them laughing and chattering away to each other in Farsi.

I hesitated in mid-thought. Is this acceptable public behavior in Teheran, Isfahan, or some other Iranian city? Do the people who live in these communities ignore the same public health issues we have been alerted to in the

West? Does anyone, other than fastidious Americans, worry about the germs, viruses, and bacteria being transmitted to the world around them? Could these two youngsters dressed in the uniform of American gang members (baggy shorts, graffiti-filled T-shirts, baseball caps turned backwards) be following patterns learned from their parents and common to Persian culture?

Then I remembered the last baseball game I had seen on television. The screen was constantly being filled with a blizzard of spitting—tobacco juice, sunflower seeds, real or imagined excess saliva—showering the dugout floor and the field between pitches. Maybe they were following *American*, rather than *Persian*, cultural patterns!

No matter now. As they started to cross the street, I treated them to a lesson in the kind of expressive English I learned in the Army from seasoned drill sergeants. In so many expletive-laced words, I told them that if they couldn't learn manners and how to respect their neighborhood as they would their own homes, they should move to a garbage dump, where they obviously belonged. Whether they understood all the words, they could not mistake the tone of my voice. They kept on moving and didn't turn back until nearly a block away.

When they did look around, I wanted them to know that I was watching them, still seething from their behavior. Then one more thought flashed through my mind and I relaxed: Why is spitting a constant part of baseball but almost never seen in professional basketball, football, and soccer games?

That got me thinking positively again. Spitting isn't an indoor/outdoor thing because football and soccer, like baseball, are also almost exclusively played in the open air. Maybe it's an educational thing. Most American basketball, football, and soccer players reach the professional level after playing for university teams, while most baseball players tend to start professionally as soon as they reach high school age.

Perhaps it has to do more with tradition. Baseball involves a lot of standing around and waiting; players chewed tobacco for its stimulative effects as well as to have something to occupy their time. Spitting is a natural outcome of chewing tobacco and is its most important associated ritual. (*Swallowing* tobacco-laced saliva is definitely not a recommended alternative.) Basket-ball, football, and soccer, on the other hand, are a lot more active and involve constant running. This leaves almost no time or place for engaging in the same ritual.

All of this suggests that *situational behavior* does indeed play a larger role in our lives than most of us realize. In other words, we tend to adjust elements of our behavior to the place and circumstances in which we find ourselves.

SITUATIONAL BEHAVIOR

SITUATIONAL BEHAVIOR

Situational behavior is our cultural message board. It is what is expected of kids and adults alike according to where they are and what is being done:

- If invited to a ceremony at the White House, males are expected to wear coat and tie. Other than an occasional exhibitionist and nonconformist, nearly everyone knows and accepts the standard. If invited to a day at a beach club in Malibu, the same person would also know to leave the coat and tie at home in favor of shorts and a sports shirt.^

- For a Davis Cup tie, the attitude on behavior is well known to tennis *aficionados*. Cheer and jeer whenever you want; stomp and jump all you want; hoist a flag, wave a towel, or hold up a sign as often as you want. But what about a *college* tennis match? Spectators would be appalled if anyone exhibited the same behavior even if it involved the same players in the same sport in the same stadium.

- Take a library? The standards are again different, but no less clear. Everyone is taught from an early age to be as quiet as possible so as not to disturb the other people reading and writing at the tables or in the stacks.

- How about communicating strong emotions? We know that to express strong emotions, we need to "speak passionately and forthrightly." But "to break bad news...we lower our voices and choose our words carefully." A rapper named Bow Wow was asked how he reacts to being called a dog." If I'm playing ball, I'd take it as an insult. But if someone...said 'Yo, what's up, dog?' I don't take that as a negative."

- Got tickets to a rock concert? When the show begins, move as the music moves you and don't stop until the stage lights go dark and the house lights come up. Got tickets to a symphony orchestra? People know to move as little as possible until the stage lights dim and the house lights come up.

We are exposed to the nuances of situational behavior almost from the first day we leave our homes with our parents.

Situational behavior defines what is considered by society to be appropriate conduct in nearly every circumstance.

It is a vital part of growing up. Parents demand an understanding of it in the home; teachers demand it at school; cops demand it on the street; ministers demand it in church; and bosses demand it at work. So why shouldn't grandparents demand it whenever they are with their grandchildren in public, on their own or with others? We believe they should! Yet we find some grandparents are afraid to enforce their understanding of correct situational behavior for fear of offending the parents, being accused of interfering in the grandchildren's lives, or changing the dynamics of family relationships. Nonsense.

Every occasion on which *Generation 1* (the grandparents) are together with *Generation 2* (the parents) and/or *Generation 3* (the grandchildren) are occasions that can move the culture seamlessly from the present into the future.^ We also believe that grandparents have an absolute responsibility to show their grandkids—by example and by explanation—how to react appropriately to each situation as it arises.

- Say you invite one of your granddaughter to have lunch with you in a restaurant. After taking the order, the waitress brings a basket of bread. As soon as it is set down, your grandchild's arm flashes out to snare a roll without a by-your-leave to anyone else at the table. Manners acceptable at home or to the grandchild's parents, perhaps, but not what *you* may want to see when you are with her in a restaurant. What might you do or say to your grandchild about appropriate manners to meet your responsibilities to the larger society in which both you and the grandchild are living?

- Take a ride in an elevator. You and your seven-year-old grandson enter together. On the way down, the elevator stops at the second floor and a woman enters. When the car reaches the lobby and the door begins to open, your grandson pushes forward to be the first out. You instinctively reach out to restrain him to allow the woman to exit first. Is this type of courtesy still appropriate in a world of equality and woman's liberation?

We won't reflect on these questions quite yet. They are dealt with in the chapter entitled "Situations and Solutions." Suffice it to say here that if you believe grandparents have a responsibility to help build and maintain a society that *they* will be happy living in, then showing a grandchild what *they* consider to be proper behavior ought not wait for the intervention of Mom or Dad. The behavior needs to be dealt with by the grandparent on the spot and at the point of occurrence.

While we believe that grandparents can indeed insist on a certain level of deportment from their grandchildren when they are with them, we also believe that the grandparents must explain two fundamental things about life and society from *their* perspective:

1. **Intervention has occurred because the grandparents want to make *their* world better.**

2. **Intervention is not intended to make the grandkids *better*—although perhaps that will occur.**

In addition, the grandkids have to be told that the demands of their grandparents for specific behavior in specific situations are only those that their *grandparents* think are appropriate. The point should be made often and clearly:

Grandparents are not declaring that there

is *necessarily* a universally accepted RIGHT or WRONG way to handle every situation as it occurs—only that there is usually the GRANDPARENTS' way of doing things.

But that can be enough to make a lasting impression on a grandchild. Show him or her your solution to specific situations and they will soon develop a body of knowledge to use for their own later independent decisions.

The key is not that you are making a grandchild's life miserable by enforcing some archaic standards, only that you are seeking to make *your* life more comfortable. We hold that you have as much right to a comfortable existence in your own community as anyone else; by the same token, we hold that no one, especially your own grandchild, has a right to make you—or anyone else— *uncomfortable* in that community.

We noted before that grandparents don't have much to do with getting the role they eventually are asked to fill; it simply is in the cards dealt to them in life and tends to come with the territory once their own kids get married.

But remember this: People become grandparents only by good fortune. It is not something they can apply for or do anything about achieving.

They can express their desire, they can explain what a new generation means, they can conduct a family poll, they can even shout from the rooftops. None of this, of course, really helps. Grandparenting comes when nature or their kids consciously decide to start a new family.

In short, the title of *GRANDPARENT* is not earned; it is thrust upon those who receive it. Much as it is with the royal family in England, the duties come with the office, whether an individual likes it or not.^ So once a person has the rank and title of *GRANDPARENT*, he or she must start thinking about how to fulfill the responsibilities that are associated with the office.

It is not up to the kids to determine how their parents should conduct themselves as grandparents. While the kids may want their parents to transform their home into a full-time day-care center, serve as unpaid babysitters on demand, or run a free limousine service to school, church, doctors, lessons, meetings, and friends, they cannot *dictate* what their parents do to fulfill their new role as grandparents. Where are the rules of grandparenting written? Who enforces them? How do you get those rules amended if you don't like them?

SOCIETAL VALUES

SOCIETAL VALUES

While there are no *specific* rules for how to grand-parent in a modern Western society, we never-theless believe that those who are grandparents have a distinctive role to play. Indeed, we think the fulfillment of the role is crucial to the sur-vival of every culture.

Start with simple etiquette. Judith Martin, fa-mously known as *Miss Manners,* notes: "Most parents are not teaching their children the man-ners they need—from 13-year-old single moth-ers on crack to corporate executives who feel the limited time with their children should be pleas-ant, so they don't ask them to do anything."^

Similarly concerned with what he observed, the chairman of United Technologies published a 1984 advertisement in *The Wall Street Journal* lamenting the fact that common courtesy in the society has gone missing:

Someone once asked a Southerner, "Where...the South actually begins?" The Southerner said... "When you notice the children say, 'Yes, Sir' and 'No, Ma'am.'" But good manners are not a matter of geography. There are as many polite children in Caribou, Maine, Wichita, Kansas, and Tacoma, Washington, as there are in Natchez, Mississippi. They don't learn politeness from a postmark."

The ad urges *parents* to make common courtesy outside of the home a common virtue again. We argue that if parents are unwilling or unable to teach their kids these and other virtues, grandparents need to take up the slack for the sake of a better society.

From our point of view, the responsibilities that come to a person who assumes the role of a grandparent start from the moment the grandchild is born and do not cease so long as the grandparent is capable of communicating.

A central part of the responsibilities of grandparenting is recognizing that they might be the primary source for transmitting *societal values* to Generation 3.

Societal values can be identified all around us. They exist in the attitudes, behaviors, activities, and priorities exhibited in a community. One man expressed these values to his family this way: "[T]he perfect balance of time [is] 25% for...family life, ...25% for business...[and] 50% of the time [for the community.] Life becomes fuller if you give more."

Some societal values—courtesy, respect, honesty—are found in what we expect from other individuals as part of our daily lives; other values become important when members of groups perceive problems. What are some of these larger values? Here is a partial list, but readers are free to add whatever issues are important to them:

- Good public schools
- A workable road system
- A variety of museums
- A wide-reaching library system
- Recreation facility for every interest
- Honest and efficient policing
- Fast response fire fighters and paramedics
- An honest currency and exchange system
- Comprehensive health care professionals

Defining exactly what is meant by "workable" or "comprehensive" is not important here. Every grandparent will have his or her own view of what constitutes a *suitable* variety of museums or whether the headquarters collection, branch system, and mobile services of the local public library are *adequate*.

But societal values are also more than what may be decided by an official organization. They can also consist of important ideas and beliefs such as:

- Freedom of speech, religion, assembly, press, movement, and more
- The right to quiet, privacy, security, and more
- The opportunity to find a job and to earn enough from it to pay for the necessities of life including food, medicine, clothing, transportation, housing, and more
- A society where all races, ethnicities, religions, and nationalities hold equal status

How these come to a society and how society makes sure that one person's version of liberty does not impinge on another's are again beyond the scope of this book. For those who may want more on any of these topics, every aspect of each issue can be heard most weekdays on dozens of talk radio shows.

By the same token, the values a society holds dear do not have to be solely political or philosophical in nature. What is important to a grandparent about preserving in his or her community and what he or she may want to convey to a grandchild can certainly have a lot lighter tone without losing any of its importance. For example:

- Strawberries—May they get bigger, cheaper, and tastier.
- Locksmiths—May they always be there to save us from our own folly.
- Bestseller lists—May we always have some idea of what others are reading.
- Supermarkets—May we have at least one that remains open 24-hours-a-day in our neighborhood.
- Fireworks—May we have at least one show a year when they light the sky and dazzle our senses.
- Immigrants—May they continue to arrive to provide new energy and add fresh cultural stimulation to our cities.
- Roses—May they always offer beauty and variety to our lives.
- Grammar—May acceptable standards of English never be subordinated to political correctness.

- Discounts—May they continue to remove some of the guilt when we spend on things we really don't need.
- Clouds—May they always float through the sky on journeys of intrigue and importance.

Looking at the little things about our society is just as significant to some as the big ticket items we worry about: Corruption, pollution, selfishness, telemarketing, scams, spam, and more. By the same token, there are some who believe that what have been called "habits of the heart" are the kind of core values that every society needs to encourage. What are these?

- Sensitivity
- Thoughtfulness
- Kindness
- Empathy
- Compassion
- Decency
- Integrity

In other words, if everyone in a community learned and practiced being *sensitive* to the needs of others and always acted toward others with *kindness*, the political issues could probably be settled very smoothly with the support of a majority of the community.

But there are still other ways to look at societal values to impart to grandchildren. A grandparent can see aspects of our society that are bothersome and that call for immediate attention to make the community a better place in which to live. For example, look at the impact of the following issues:

- The search for more and more corporate profits and higher and higher stock market prices
- Excessive personal rewards for the leadership of nonprofit organizations as justification for retaining their employment
- Blackmarket merchants who rationalize their sale of guns and drugs with words that imply that if they didn't do it, someone else would
- Lawyers on the prowl for cases against institutions with such deep pockets that they might settle a matter rather than argue its merits in court
- Drivers who act as if no other vehicle has a right to interfere with the progress they wish to make on the road
- Headquarter offices that have an overblown concept of their worth to the overall success of an organization.

- Jingoistic supporters of capitalism who refuse to see what others believe are its cruelties and deficiencies
- Union officials who treat any criticism of a member or policy as an assault on the entire institution of organized labor
- Any individual who cheats, robs, or assaults with no remorse for the disruption and devastation caused the victim
- Self-righteous individuals who complain bitterly about someone else's malfeasance, all the while protecting some questionable arrangement of their own
- Pharmaceutical houses who look for extracurricular means to influence doctors to prescribe their medicines
- Doctors who righteously claim that the extracurricular activities of pharmaceutical houses cannot influence their professional judgments

This list, too, is endless, but you get the idea that it takes very little effort to establish any individual's litany of what is wrong with society or what needs to be done to make it better. Once these societal values *are* established, though, they form the basis of our culture and the foundation of our communities.

In short, *societal values* are the expectations each of us has about the assumptions others will make and the actions others will take. Collectively, the sum total of this behavior becomes the basis of our civilization.

Reinforcing or tweaking the established values of society becomes even more important when we become grandparents. In our view, grandparents have a responsibility to transmit accurate expectations of the community to their grandchildren. We believe it is a responsibility that devolves on grandparents when they assume the title.

Like many other things in life, the responsibilities of grandparenting exists beyond any parental powers to control them. Most people forget how many outsiders are already looking over a parent's shoulder—the schools, courts, police, child welfare officials. They also forget how many others, such as peers, coaches, mentors, troop leaders, and radio personalities are constantly talking to kids with different ideas on what to think or how to act.

There are also real reasons for caring about the society around us. Take the example of the United

States. Although economically powerful, militarily unassailable, and technologically dominant at the present time, it has not achieved all that it could and has not yet become the "shining city on the hill" in the words of its founders. Dr. Kevin Ryan at Boston University's School of Ethics puts it this way:

> *One of the greatest threats to [America's] current good fortune and [its] future prosperity is the widespread failure of the adult community...to pass on to young people the core moral values which are the foundation of a good life and a good society.*

Ryan goes on to note that many kids have a poor grasp of such universally accepted virtues as "responsibility, respect, self-control, and honesty." He points out that a recent study of 8,600 high schools students found that:

- *Cheating* is widespread. More than 70 percent admitted to cheating on an examination; 45 percent indicated that they did it often.
- *Lying* is rampant. A staggering 92 percent of students said they had lied to their parents in the previous 12 months and nearly 80 percent indicated that they did it often.

- *Drinking* is prevalent. About 16 percent of kids admitted to having been drunk *in* school and nearly 10 percent indicated it had happened two or more times.

The author of the study referred to the "shocking level of moral illiteracy" among American students and noted that it represented what he called the thinning of the "moral ozone." To be sure, this may not be the sole fault of today's parents; the grandparents may have failed them in this area as well.

The Partnership for a Drug-Free America echoes the same concerns in calling on *grandparents* to discuss the danger of drugs openly with their grandchildren. Why? Because, the Partnership notes:

> "The average age of first-time drug use among teens is 13. Some kids start at 9. Roughly 15% of American kids between 9 and 12 are offered illegal drugs. And 30% of these kids receive the offer from a friend. Illegal drugs can be linked to increased violence in many communities, to AIDS, to birth defects, drug-related crime, and homelessness.

Recognizing the standing that grandparents have with their grandchildren, the Partnership urges the use of what it calls grandparenting "power as an influencer to steer grandchildren away from drugs."

But in a telling revelation of how little respect grandparents are really given in defining and enforcing societal values in the U.S. today, the Partnership invites grandparents to send for "information on how to talk to your grandkids about drugs. Just ask for your free copy of 'A *Parent's* Guide to Prevention.'" (Emphasis added.)

You would think that if the Partnership could put upwards of $100,000 into the creation and publication of their advertisements to get grandparents involved in freeing America of drugs, they could afford to update and reprint their pamphlet to one that recognizes the differences between the roles played by parents and grandparents in the lives of *Generation 3*. How much money and effort would it have taken to create "A *Grandparent's* Guide to Preventing Drug Abuse"?

To what extent attitudes on cheating, lying, drinking, and drugs—and their consequent actions— arise within a family setting is the source of a fierce debate. Some in our society hold parents solely responsible for how their kids react in public; others want to blame permissive schools, soft prosecutors, a lax movie rating system, spineless advertisers, Internet pornography, cable television, bi-coastal liberals of every possible stripe, Dr. Spock, and a dozen other "usual suspects." Our view is the following:

How children act in a family setting, the values they adopt, the belief system they accept, and the attitudes they exhibit at home remain the sole province of their parents.

But since all kids eventually leave their homes, and their attitudes and actions play out in the public arena, anyone in that arena has a right to intervene on behalf of the larger society. For whatever reasons we have come to this pass, we think we ought not have to have to nag at single parents or retrain elementary school teachers or pass new laws in the legislature to get better behavior from the next generation. Rather, we think that the grandparenting generation exists as an important resource to make our communities better places for all of us to enjoy.

In fact, we are arguing here that grandparents have an *obligation* to help their grandchildren understand and appreciate the world around them. By virtue of their age and experience, grandparents by definition have to have a different perspective than that of their own children. They have been around longer; they have seen more. If nothing else, they may have served in the military—with its more rigid expectations of behavior—while their kids may not have. As a result, grandparents have a duty to communicate what they know, what they have observed, and what they feel to their grandchildren—as sensitively as is humanly possible.

That being said, many newly minted grandparents would agree with Gail Sheehy on how the title should be accepted and how their new office should be conducted:

"In this role [of grandparenting], we are meant to give support, not advice. Our most important function is simple: To be present."

As Sheehy heard from one grandmother she interviewed: "The surprise for me is not being on the front lines anymore. I can just watch the show."

We clearly think the Sheehy interpretation of the role of grandparenting falls short. We think our society is wasting a rich resource in letting grandparents get away with *observer* status only. By standing on the sidelines, grandparents are also abdicating a responsibility that society needs performed—to be sure Generation 3 understands appropriate behavior in every possible public setting.

We see the role of grandparenting as essentially the same no matter the age of the grandkids or their physical location. In our view the *role* doesn't change, only the way in which the role is fulfilled is altered by circumstances.

The remainder of this book, then, is about assisting you in finding ways to fulfill that role more effectively. Our ideas are meant to be illustrative, not comprehensive, in nature; we merely want to suggest how various events can be handled and stimulate you into thinking how you might handle related circumstances.

SITUATIONS AND SOLUTIONS

AT THE MALL

THE SITUATION

You have gone to the local mall to pick up a pair of glasses on the way to taking one of your grandkids back to his home. As soon as you are inside the mall, the little boy spots one of the stationary trains in front of a fastfood outlet and starts begging for a ride. Several things flash through your mind: (1) You really don't have the time; (2) You really hate to be manipulated the way you have seen the youngster play his mother (your daughter);^ and (3) You don't want a big scene when you say no.

THE SOLUTION

If you were lucky, you might have anticipated the request and explained that there isn't enough time before the grandchild even saw the ride. If you weren't, we would explain to the grandchild that some events are dictated by an adult need, some things are governed by a child's desires. This trip is to fulfill an adult requirement. The next time an activity for the grandchild can be included in the plan. Write the promise down, find a date on the calendar when you can make a return trip to the mall, and make sure your grandkid knows when you do keep the promise you made.

---

^ See footnote on p. 12 for an explanation of the carat mark.

IN THE ARENA

THE SITUATION

You decide to take the grandkids to the circus. The parents are delighted, the kids are excited, and you are thrilled at the chance of reliving your memories of a bigtop circus. But just as soon as the lights dim and the first eye-popping group of performers appeares on the arena floor, your youngest grandkid complains he can't see and doesn't want to sit on your lap. No, he announces very loudly, he wants to stand on his seat. When you whisper that it will block the view of the people behind, he hisses that his parents always let him do it!

THE SOLUTION

Rather than debate the issue at that moment and at that time, simply ask the child to come with you to the manager's office to see if the facility provides booster seats. In this way, both of you are working on a mutually acceptable solution without arguing the merits of what his parents allow—if they do, in fact, let him stand on theater seats whenever he wants. As you head down the stairs and out the passageway, turn back to show the child that if all else fails you may be able to watch the rest of the show from that vantage point. If you do and he gets tired, you can always suggest that you return to your seats because he may be able to see better than he first thought.

AT LAS VEGAS NIGHT

THE SITUATION

The whole family has been invited to a party where the event coordinator has arranged gambling games for the entertainment. Your grandkids love to gamble when they are with you. When you see the painted horses standing in a corner, you explain that people will choose a "horse" they think will win, buying or receiving a ticket to show their support. Two dice will be rolled. The red die determines the number of the horse; the blue indicates how many squares the horse can move. Everyone is eager to participate in this game, but you remember what a stranger said to you one evening in 1948 on the *SS Mauretania*. You decide to tell the story to the grandkids

THE SOLUTION

The man saw how I burned for number 4 to win. I had bet a pound—my entire allowance—and was desperate to get £5 for winning. When the ship's officer announced two to move three spaces, I was miserable—and my face showed the pain; when he said four could go six, I was ecstatic. The stranger whispered: "When you want something so much for yourself that you wish ill of others, you will never enjoy the victory; when you really want to share your good fortune with others, it will always come to you." A good lesson never forgotten and worthy of sharing.

IN A RESTAURANT—PART A

THE SITUATION

After giving your order to the waitress, she brings a basket of hot rolls tucked under a gleaming white napkin. The instant the basket hits the table, your granddaughter swoops in. She throws back the cover and snags a roll. Before she can start buttering it, though, you lean toward her to ask her to stop. Whisper that you have something more important than rolls for her.

THE SOLUTION

Tell her it is a secret that you learned a long time ago: One of our great blessings is to be able to help others before we help ourselves. It shows that we care about them as much as we care about ourselves. That makes our world a nicer place. When people are selfish, others may not be there to help when help is needed...and absolutely everyone *needs help at some time in his or her life. Ask your granddaughter if she has ever needed help? Then explain that at a restaurant the best thing to do is* pass *the bread or anything else meant for everyone. It shows that you are strong enough to wait and that you care about the well-being and health of others. Tell your granddaughter to try it and see how much it will be appreciated by everyone else at the table.*

IN A RESTAURANT—PART B

THE SITUATION

This is the same situation as the previous one—a waitress brings some rolls, your granddaughter swoops in to snare a piece under the covering napkin as soon as the basket hits the table—but instead of being on your own, her parents (your son and daughter-in-law) are along. Neither her mother nor her father has said a word about the behavior. This time restrain your granddaughter gently from starting the buttering process while whispering to her parents that you are going to tell your granddaughter a secret and then share it with them.

THE SOLUTION

The secret, of course, is the same—it is a blessing to be able to help others before helping ourselves. Once you have asked your granddaughter to pass the basket, turn to her parents to tell them what you told her: When we care about others as much as we care about ourselves, the world becomes a nicer place. When people are selfish, others may not be there to help them when help is needed. Ask your son and daughter-in-law to show their appreciation to their daughter for the strength and concern she has just displayed. Note that by bringing the parents into the exchange with the grandchild before and *after the incident is handled, the chances of noses getting out of joint or charges of interference should be greatly diminished.*

IN THE ELEVATOR

THE SITUATION

Your are with your two grandchildren in a doctors' building waiting for an elevator. The kids have already had an argument over who gets to push the down button for the car and then choose the parking garage indicator. The elevator starts its decent, stops, and two older people enter. The man is maneuvering a walker and the woman is juggling her handbag and a pile of X-ray envelopes. As the door opens at the garage level, the kids push past each other and the couple in a mad dash to be first out. You are appalled, apologize profusely, and then dart out to make sure the kids cannot get into any danger on their own.

THE SOLUTION

Once in your car, you tell the kids to pay attention. What they did when they left the elevator was both thoughtless and dangerous. Instead of rushing out, wouldn't it have been better to make sure the door stayed open so the older couple could exit? Instead of seeing who could find the car first, wouldn't it have been nicer to ask the lady if she needed help carrying her X rays? Now instead of driving off, go back to the elevator. Show the kids the OPEN DOOR symbol; rehearse a polite way to ask if someone needs help. Perhaps take a ride for practice. A societal value exposed. Responsibility met!

59

IN THE MUSEUM

THE SITUATION

A special exhibit of objects made from ivory is planned for your city's principal art museum. Your granddaughter is old enough to appreciate the experience and you certainly want to go. You make a date with her parents, order the tickets, and depart. As you enter the first gallery, you realize that she won't be able to see a thing because of all the adults hovering around the display cases. Your back is not strong enough to hoist her up each time and yet you want her to see what you came for.

THE SOLUTION

There are several. My favorite is to go to the Museum Shop to review a display copy of the catalog for the show. Look through all the items to decide the 10 you most want to see. Write down the description, then ask one of the guards where you can find each. Once in the proper gallery, you and your granddaughter merely wait in the crowd around one of the objects you have selected to view. Once you have worked your way to the front, spend as much time as you need to study and discuss the piece. When done, move to the next. Eventually, let your granddaughter do the waiting while you sit watching for her signal to come forward. It will prove to have been a memorable experience.

IN THE CAR

THE SITUATION

The grandkids have come with snacks for the long drive to an amusement park. Not 10 minutes after getting under way, one of them opens a package of potato chips; you silently wonder if your portable vacuum will be strong enough to clean up the crumbs. As your mind returns to the road, you feel a blast of air as a back window opens and the empty package whips noisily out. You are outraged and embarrassed. You decide it is better for your blood pressure and your relationship with your grandkids if you deal with the littering issue immediately.

THE SOLUTION

On the road's shoulder, the offender simply whines, "What?" "Throwing that bag out was disrespectful of everyone else who drives this highway. Besides, a cop could have fined me $100," you say evenly. "Well," responds the kid defiantly, "my mother always has a litterbag in the car. Where's yours?" Perfect. An invitation to a lesson in situational behavior. "We don't have one; never have. We drop our car trash off every time we stop. Something we had to do growing up when there was no weekly garbage pickup. As a result, we learned to generate a lot less trash. Better for the environment. Remember, it's our way on the highway. Please just accept that whenever you are in the car with us."

AFTER AN ACCIDENT

THE SITUATION

You have been invited to use the facilities of an absent friend's beach house. A brief lecture to the grandkids as you approach: "It is a very special privilege to be able to use this house whenever we come to the beach—somewhere to change and clean up and to leave our things. We have to be very careful not to disturb anything and to leave the house as clean and neat as when we arrive." Naturally, as soon as the door is opened, one of the kids stumbles into a table, knocking a photo off. A chip from the corner of the wooden frame flies across the floor. Not the least chagrined by his clumsiness, the little boy announces: "I'll look for some glue."

THE SOLUTION

Explain that this is not how you want to handle the situation. Might not be the kid's way or the parents' way, but it is your *way. That's what counts when the interests of your friends are involved. Ask the kid to look for a piece of paper, not glue. Tell him he is going to write a note of remorse to the owner and that you will write a note explaining that you will find a replacement frame. Situation handled, lesson imparted.*

IN THE HOTEL

THE SITUATION

You are taking your two kids and their five grandchildren away for a vacation. You decide on a resort hotel with all the facilities at hand—swimming pool, spa, putting green, tennis courts, game room, gymnasium, snack bar, dining room, shops, Nintendo games, on-demand movies, and more. You assume that since you are "in the chair" (paying for the holiday) as the English would say, your rules of behavior will apply in this situation. But moments after the bellman puts everyone in his proper room, the kids are out in the hall pounding up and down and looking for the soda machine. The parents are no where in sight.

THE SOLUTION

Latching on to one of the kids, you ask him to round up his siblings, his cousins, and all of the parents for an immediate pow wow in the grandparents' room. Once everyone is assembled, you explain that hundreds of other people are at this resort, that everyone there has to abide by a set of rules concerning noise, motion, cleanliness, and more to avoid chaos. The rules are based on making sure that what you are doing does not bother anyone else. If in doubt, ask those around you. If not sure, ask one of the adults in the family. If they are not available, ask one of the hotel staff. Remind the grandkids that in these situations the "askor" bestows a mantle of authority and flatters the "askee," thus enhancing their own status.

63

IN THE MIDDLE OF THE LOBBY

THE SITUATION

You are on your way to the elevator bank to go up to the 9th floor to drop off a document needed by your attorney. Your grandson is along for company. As you cross the building lobby, you see a drop-dead gorgeous young lady in a tailored pink suit set off by a large matching hat. Your first instinct is that you have landed in the middle of a fashion shoot; your second is to remember the days when every woman left the house dressed in a similar way. All three of you end up waiting for the elevator together. Do you just stay with your thoughts or should you turn the situation into a learning lesson for your grandson?

THE SOLUTION

We believe that leading by example is one of the best ways to teach others. Our habit has always been to pay a compliment if someone deserves recognition, so we would probably have turned to the young lady to say something along the lines of: "You have to go to the Kentucky Derby these days to have an outfit like you're wearing fully appreciated." If she seems put off by your comment, apologize for the intrusion; if she thanks you for the compliment, accept her words with a smile and a nod. Either way, share your impressions of her reaction with your grandson to reinforce the lesson of how nice it feels to make occasional and appropriate contact with strangers in an otherwise impersonal urban society.

IN FRONT OF THE DRUGSTORE

THE SITUATION

After parking the car, you herd three grandkids in front of you on your way to collecting a prescription at the drugstore. A very dirty creature looks up from where he had been dozing in a corner to say that he's thirsty and hungry and wants to get some milk. You see the wine bottle and cigarette butts near him. You doubt that he's the milk and cookie type, but you have to admire how he was playing off the kids to get money from you. What lessons can be drawn from this situation? How can a situation like this best be handled?

THE SOLUTION

Some will instinctively react to such a request by coolly ignoring it, while others will want to put space between themselves and the stranger. Some will offer $1 or $2, explaining to the kids that giving alms to beggars has biblical status. Others will use an informational approach that can turn a potentially uncomfortable confrontation into a learning experience by asking the guy some questions—his name, how long he has been out of work, does he know where the homeless shelter is? Later you can talk to the kids about the situation and perhaps explain how to tell the difference between professional beggars and those who really need help—professional beggars are usually relentless in hounding you for money while those who need help tend to ask once and hope for the best.)

ON THE STREET

THE SITUATION

You are on the way to get your grandson an ice cream. As you approach the corner, the light is already green. Like a powerful puppy straining at the restrictions of his leash, your grandchild is tugging at your hand to hurry. But knee surgery a year ago makes quick movements impossible. In fact, you have made a rule that you cross only on a fresh green light to be sure to give yourself plenty of time. It is a good time to impart one of your favorite societal precepts: A good society—the kind you want to live in and the kind you hope your kids and grandkids will want to live in—is one in which everyone, at every age, is looking out for everyone else.

THE SOLUTION

Instead of pulling back or even explaining why you don't feel comfortable crossing at that point, tell him that you want to play a game. Ask him to tell you all the possible dangers he sees around him...something that could hurt you or others as well as him. Tell him that being patient and waiting to cross on a new green light is his way of protecting you and that if he and his friends always look to protect themselves and others from danger, we will all live in a safer world.

ON THE TELEPHONE

THE SITUATION

You decide to call your grandchild to talk about his science project. Perhaps you can help with the expenses or give him some ideas. As soon as he greets you, his younger brother starts trying to pull the phone away, saying *he* wants to talk with Grandpa; you hear them begin to fight and argue—on your credit card. Then your daughter-in-law starts yelling in the background to take a message, she's busy, and she'll have to phone back, never dreaming that the call might be for one of the kids.

THE SOLUTION

Create a signal with your grandchildren whenever they are losing concentration on what you are saying. It could be a special code word or two (BUZZ, ZIP IT, FOCUS) or a signal (an index finger in the air, making a T for time-out, a snap of the fingers). The kids are told that whenever they hear or see that signal they must immediately stop *whatever they are doing to pay absolute attention to you. You have to explain and reiterate that the signal could be given because of an emergency situation, an urgent matter of timing, a matter of courtesy, or something else. Once you establish the signal, use it. The kids will accept it as something that comes with the territory of being involved with their grandparents.*

AT A FUNERAL

THE SITUATION

You have arranged to take your grandson to a nearby ski resort on Thursday of the following week when seniors receive a 50 percent discount on lift tickets. Both of you are looking forward to the chance to be together. Then you learn that a good friend—your weekly tennis partner—had a heart attack and died. His funeral is that Thursday. You call your daughter-in-law, tell her that you have been asked to give the eulogy, and want to take your grandson along rather than cancel your chance to be together.

THE SOLUTION

While your daughter-in-law always hates to disappoint her son, she is very hesitant; she hasn't talked to him much about death, knows that he will vehemently protest having to wear something other than shorts and tennis shoes, and remembers how uncomfortable she felt at her first funeral. You suggest that funerals are a part of life that your grandson needs to learn; that perhaps her discomfort arose because no one had told her what to expect; that seeing adults cry is no different than seeing an infant cry—both are using tears to deal with the uncertainty and insecurity of the moment; that participating in a social ritual honoring someone's memory is part of the continuum that moves civilization from the present to the future. You ask her to reconsider on the grounds that a positive experience at a funeral will stand him in good stead for a lifetime.

MEETING THE MAN

THE SITUATION

You are taking your granddaughter with you to meet a local member of the House of Representatives. You think she will benefit from seeing a part of the political process in action. You also want to show her how people should use the system before feeling the need to go outside of it to get something done. You and she have discussed what questions she might ask. You introduce her to the Congressman, he comes right back by quizzing her on her plans for college, and she ends up just shrugging. "There's time, Congressman," you say. "She's not in high school yet!" Then without hesitating, you ask him the questions *you* had prepared.

THE SOLUTION

Afterwards, tell your granddaughter that rehearsing conversations in your mind is good preparation for various contingencies. Remind her that you knew what questions you would ask long before arriving. Point out that it often isn't the answer *that counts but the fact that a topic was raised. It reminds the politician that it is something important to a segment of his constituency and establishes you as a key person in that segment. Bottom-line lesson: Always have a plan, try to control every occasion to your benefit, and keep track of the contacts you make for use in the future.*

ANOTHER CONVERSATION

THE SITUATION

It's a nice day and you decide to take the visiting grand-kids along on a walk-the-dog mission. After a turn around the block, you head for the local park where they can play handball against a backboard and you can watch. No sooner do you find a bench than two 20-something guys cross the path carrying on a loud conversation: "You bet your f------ a-- he knows how to play," says one. "That motherf----- would rather s--- than pass the f------ ball," answers the other. "No f------ way." The grandkids are mesmerized and start repeating the words to each other to try them on. What should you do?

THE SOLUTION

Call the kids over and explain that some people have a vocabulary problem; you call them word wimps. They know a few that are designed to shock, offend, or get attention while ignoring the other 500,000 or so that can be more expressive, more articulate, and more interesting. Remind the kids of the essence of the conversation—one guy saying that Friend A really understands basketball while the second guy disagrees, noting his selfishness as a player. Ask each grandkid to role play the conversation with the same emphasis but using different words.

THE WAITING ROOM

THE SITUATION

Your wife drops you and your grandson off at the dealership to pick up your car. You two are on your way to miniature golf and lunch. The dealership's waiting room is equipped with magazines, a TV set, and a large table covered with Lego blocks for building. You encourage your grandson to make a tower. As you watch, a much older kid comes in, plunks himself down at the table, and starts grabbing pieces from your grandson's structure. You are appalled, there is no other adult in sight, and your grandson is looking to you for help.

THE SOLUTION

We think you have four choices in a situation like this: Take your grandson away, demand the other kid stop, look for someone in authority, or find a way to get the two kids to work together. The choice you make naturally depends on the circumstances, your energy, and the amount of time available. If you were to choose the last option, you might get your grandson to ask the other boy what he wants to build or have your grandson invite the other kid to help create an even bigger tower. However you eventually decide to handle the matter, make sure your grandson understands what you did, why you did it, and the ultimate result of having done what you did.

FOR THE UNEXPECTED

THE SITUATION

You once loved to play racquetball, but since moving away from the convenience of a club where you could always get court time, you haven't played at all. Because the ball is kept in play by the surrounding walls and ceiling, it is easier for little kids to play than tennis. You think it would be fun for your out-of-town grandkids to experience and it would be fun for you as well. On the way to the club your mobile phone rings. A close friend has just been taken to the hospital after a car accident and his wife is asking you to come.

THE SOLUTION

The grandkids don't know the friend and will be disappointed at having to miss the racquetball game that had been planned for weeks. But you know you have to go directly to the hospital to assess the situation and to give whatever help you can. The parents of the grandkids are off on their own errands. What to do? Tell the truth. Tell the kids that sometimes things don't go as you want and that perhaps you can still get the racquetball game in after *going to the hospital. Remind them that one of life's most important lessons is adapting to unexpected change and how they handle the situation today will serve them for a lifetime.*

TECHNIQUES

THE TECHNIQUES

The techniques we think will help grandparents deal effectively with their responsibilities and provide the social guidance that the grandchildren can use are presented in 26 separate segments:

1. Be Brief
2. Explain It
3. Be Precise
4. Ask Questions
5. Tell the Truth
6. Be Positive
7. It's Gotta Make Sense
8. Dealingwith Dissent
9. Keep it Simple
10. Anticipation
11. Make the Time Count
12. Why?
13. Have Patience
14. Create Stories
15. Leave the Door Open
16. Get 'Em Started
17. Show 'Em
18. Everything Has Meaning
19. What's Really Important
20. For the Parents—Part A
21. For the Parents—Part B
22. For the Parents—Part C
23. It's the Adrenaline Rush
24. It's Their Time
25. Each One, Teach One
26. Relax!

1. BE BRIEF

When communicating with your grandkids in person, by phone, or on the Internet, remember to be brief. They not only don't need lectures, they won't listen to them or read them in any case.

Enough said.

2. EXPLAIN IT

Someone once explained to me why little kids tend to react differently to delays than their parents. It made sense. For a two year old, waiting 15 minutes for his mother to finish her coffee does indeed seem forever. Those 15 minutes represents *20 times* more of his young life than the same period for Mom. No wonder he can get impatient.

Recognize the difference in perspective between your grandchild and yourself. Explain why you are doing things, why you are requiring certain behavior. Never assume that something is obvious on its face. While it may be to you, it almost certainly will not be to your grandkids.

3. BE PRECISE

Ever watch a military policeman command a flow of traffic? The body language is as exacting as a flashing electronic arrow. They are trained to provide exact signals that leave no doubt about the direction, timing, and movement required. No dance steps, floppy wrists, or writhing bodies that are often the signature moves of policemen at major intersections in Caribbean countries. To the military, traffic control is business, not entertainment.

Communicating with grandchildren of any age about what you expect of them in public should be done in the same way. By your tone of voice, choice of words, and body language, indicate exactly what is wanted of them.

Remember that there is always time to have fun with your grandkids. Exercising your responsibilities, exposing them to something that you hope will register deeply in their psyches, is not that time.

4. ASK QUESTIONS

For experienced poker players, the caution is always the same: Be sure to check for aces before committing a large stake to any single hand. Those who forget this axiom do so at their peril.

No different for grandparents dealing with their grandkids. Always be sure to check that they understand the points you made and the rationale for your position. Asking directly—*Do you understand?* or *Got it?*—usually results in a desultory "Yes." A natural reaction. No one, especially a kid dealing with an adult, wants to admit that he or she wasn't paying attention or really didn't understand something.

Use the same technique with the grandkids employed by professional interrogators. Keep probing around the same theme with different questions and different approaches until you are satisfied that your grandchild really *does* get your point. To clinch it, ask the child to repeat back to you the main points you want understood.

5. TELL THE TRUTH

Whether it is a question you are asked or a piece of information you want to convey, remember to tell it, in Howard Cosell's immortal words, "like it is." Don't hedge, don't fudge, don't mess around. Just tell the truth as you see it.

As every grandparent learns, kids have an uncanny sixth sense to know when you are verbally dodging and weaving around a subject. Older kids lose trust in you; younger kids repeat your words or mimic your tone. Fibbing never works.

If you have the slightest hesitation about the impact of what you are about to say, explain that one person's certainty is another person's doubt. Truth can be elusive; it is not as definitive as some would have us believe. Watching a field goal attempt from the 50 yard line often seems as if the ball sails over the center of the crossbar. Watching the same field goal attempt from the end zone can show that the ball barely missed an upright. Truth can appear to us in the same way.

6. BE POSITIVE

There is a delightful story out of the Borscht Belt about a guest who was asked what he thought of the food at the hotel where he stayed. "It wasn't very good and besides there wasn't enough of it." After a lifetime of battling the fates, lots of people see the world in pessimistic terms.

Grandparents are no exception. Worse, their health may have begun to deteriorate which tends to exacerbate any negative thoughts they might harbor.

Suck it up. Forget about the aches and pains for a moment. How many times do you get to be with your grandchildren? Show them how to see the hopeful side of every situation you confront. At high school we had a slogan: "School Spirit Is Contagious." It was. But then again so is a positive attitude. In short, enjoy explaining why certain societal values you hold dear are important to you and how they make for a better society.

7. IT'S GOTTA MAKE SENSE

Every grandparent remembers having to fall back on an age-old rationale for wanting their kids to do something: "Because I said so, that's why!"

Still good enough for some parents, perhaps, but never good enough for *grandparents*. Grandparents are seeking to gain the trust of their grandchildren to preserve what has been developed in the past and to fix what needs correction for the future. That trust can come only when participants are open and honest with each other. It cannot come by fiat. The young ones will see the mistakes and recognize the illogic left by older generations.

In discussing what needs to be done for society, both you and your grandchildren will come to solutions that just might work in the future.

8. DEALING WITH DISSENT

It happens to every grandparent at some point. The grandkid balks at something that is important to you at a particular place, at a particular time—he doesn't want to sit still, move over, complete a task. The British call it "bloody-mindedness."

We can't tell you how to react at such a moment because every situation *is* different, but we do have a suggestion. When you are with your grandkids and fulfilling your responsibilities to impart societal values, treat them as small adults. Tell them what you expect and warn them that if they forget to wait their turn, speak softly, keep their hands to themselves, walk rather than run, or commit some other transgression you will remind them of what is appropriate. Just as you feel free to admonish adults when they suffer an attack of road rage or throw a fit in a restaurant, so you should do the same with the grandkids.

It doesn't take a falling Mosler Safe to get someone's attention. The key is to make the behavior expected absolutely clear.

9. KEEP IT SIMPLE

Every salesperson learns about **KISS**—**K**eep **I**t **S**imple, **S**tupid; advertising specialists are taught the Rule of 3—people can assimilate no more than three facts in one advertisement; designers know about the "Z" pattern—eyes move left to right across the top of a page (hence, the importance of a headline), then *diagonally* down the page (the reason for a centered illustration) to the bottom lefthand corner, where they hardly pause (a good place for reference or legal data) before racing across to the right and stopping (thus the spot to call for action).

Because background information can confuse and details can complicate, sometimes the easiest way for grandparents to KISS their grandkids is with easy-to-understand-and-remember mottos. Here are just two we like:

- TNT—TODAY, NOT TOMORROW.
- IF BETTER IS POSSIBLE, THEN GOOD IS NOT ENOUGH.^

Choose your favorite, then have it silk-screened onto a T-shirt for the grandkids.

10. ANTICIPATION

You have been there; you are a veteran at dealing with kids. How else did you get those delicious grandchildren? So you can anticipate a lot of what they may do or ask depending on the situation you put them in. Rather than fumble for an answer or debate someone else, think about how you feel when dealing with certain issues beforehand.

- Your grandchild wants a candy bar or a toy she sees in a store. You know all the reasons you used to tell your own kids NO, but you may want to make your refusal into a lesson about the world. Could it be better to buy this for someone else? Could our church use the money instead? You get the idea. Just be ready to put your answer into play.
- The little one picks up something from the ground. She starts to put it in her mouth, you scream, she jumps, and tears flow. It's not how you deal with the crying, but the way you use the occasion to make a point about good health that will last her a lifetime. Anticipate!

11. MAKE YOUR TIME COUNT

When I worked in the Executive Office of President Lyndon Johnson, I was amazed to learn that literally every moment of his daily activities was recorded. Presidential schedules are so full that devoting five hours to a single subject in a week of meetings, calls, and conversations represented a major commitment of his resources.

Because most grandparents generally come in and out of their grandchildren's lives for short bursts of time, make the time count as much as if you were president of the United States. Think through what you want to do with them before you greet them; make notes of what you want to say to them before you see them; rehearse how you can best convey something important.

It may sound laborious and perhaps stilted, but it is one of the best ways to insure that you are fulfilling your responsibilities as completely and as successfully as possible in the time available.

12. WHY?

Every grandparent soon realizes that kids ask endless questions to get to the bottom of something they have just learned. As a reminder on what it sometimes takes to satisfy that wonderful and innate curiosity, here is a story worth remembering.

The standard railroad gauge in the United States is 4 feet, 8.5 inches. An odd number, but that's the distance separating the rails in Britain, and British expatriates built the first U.S. railroads. Why did the British build them like that? Because the first rail lines were built by the same people who built the pre-railroad tramways, and that's the gauge they used. Why that gauge? Because the people who built the tramways used the same jigs and tools used for building wagons, which used that wheel spacing. Why? Because that's the spacing of the wheel ruts on England's old long-distance roads. So who built those first rutted roads? Imperial Rome. The ruts were made by their war chariots. Everyone else had to match them for fear of destroying their own wheels. So the standard railroad gauge of 4 feet, 8.5 inches, in the U.S. is actually derived from the original specifications for a Roman war chariot.^

The next time you or your grandkids puzzle over some strange, seemingly unexplainable requirement, remember that Rome's chariots were made just wide enough to accommodate the back ends of two horses!

13. HAVE PATIENCE

Grandkids ask a million questions:

- Why do Internet addresses start with www?
- How come you breathe so loudly?
- Why do you get ABC on Channel 38 when we get it on Channel 7?
- Is it really illegal for an atheist to hold office in Tennessee?
- What's an atheist?
- If the sun always rises in the east, how come my teacher says that it rises over the *Pacific Ocean* in Panama?

You won't know the answers to some of the questions, but you can show the grandkids how to find out. Pick off one question. Go to the library. Talk to the librarian. Work with your grandchild at the library's computer or in its card catalog—if it still has one. Go to the stacks and find some books to see if you can find the answer. You may not come up with anything more than speculation, but the entire exercise will have been fun, the grandchild will never forget the experience, and a lesson for life will have been learned.

14. CREATE STORIES

Kids relate to stories, especially animal stories. If you can find an aspect of animal behavior that matches a point you want to make with your grandkids, do so. They will understand and they will remember.

Adults do the same. Everyone who has heard about Pavlov's dogs can describe the main parameters of the experiment and how the dogs reacted.

Besides it may be a good excuse to get away from having to watch cartoons on television with your grandchildren. The Discovery Channel and other cable channels that specialize in programs devoted to animal behavior may give you and your grandchildren good ideas and easier ways to communicate. Check the programs out; record something you think may be of interest to both Generation 1 and Generation 3.

15. LEAVE THE DOOR OPEN

Sometimes we hear something that makes a lot of sense to us at the time. Fine. But before imparting this wisdom as immutable fact, be sure to leave some room for possible change.

Example: In the 1950s, we learned that nearly all birds choose mates for life. Now DNA analysis shows that chicks in the nest can actually have multiple parents—from 0 percent in snow geese to 90 percent in Australian fairy wren. In short, the behavior we see in other animals—changing skin color to match their surroundings—may not work for us and basic behaviors we share, such as parenting and a craving for sugar, may not provide much guidance for us.^

Humans have chosen to live in societies shaped by rules, not nature's laws. Murder is condemned among humans because it is destabilizing, even though intra-species killing is common in the rest of the animal kingdom. That's why an understanding of societal values, tempered by changing circumstances, is so important.

16. GET 'EM STARTED

How do we make a better community? It won't happen because grandparents decree it or grandkids wish it. It happens with hard work. Here are some ideas to get your grandkids working with you to improve things around you:

- Volunteer with your grandkids for a community project—collecting waste oil, cleaning up a vacant lot, painting a building, removing grafitti. If your local paper doesn't list these kinds of events, call city hall. The mayor's office will know.
- Sit down with your grandkids to help them draft a letter to a politician praising something or asking for something. Letters count and helping kids write them can be important in their future.
- Persistence counts as much as hard work. Harry Truman told Dwight Eisenhower that presidents can make a demand, but things get done only after you have explained it, traded for it, or raised the issue so often that the bureaucrats will do it to get you off their backs.

17. SHOW 'EM

I have written or co-authored five books on how to stimulate word of mouth advertising. In one of them, I had an idea for non-profit groups. I explained it this way:

A few years ago, the Alzheimer's Association in Chicago sent me a birthday card with a blank space and this following wording:

Happy Birthday 1998
- - - -

In commemoration of your birthday, I have given financial support to the Alzheimer's Association's Ronald & Nancy Reagan Research Institute.

Nice idea. My wife's birthday was coming in a few days and I wasn't sure she would like the present I had purchased, so I wrote "Dear Barbara" at the top, signed it in the space provided, and made a donation in her name to the charity. Only later did I realize that the birthday card had been meant to be presented to former President Reagan for *his* birthday. Given my reaction to the solicitation, I thought the Alzheimer folks were missing a better and broader variation on the idea—present birthday cards (and matching envelopes) that can be filled out and sent to those celebrating a birthday, along with donation cards to be sent back to the charity's Chicago headquarters.

Why not introduce young grandchildren to the joys of giving in a similar way. Arrange with a local charity to make a donation and obtain stickers, pins, and literature in return. Ask your young relative to pass these out to his or her friends, thus spreading the word on the charity's work.

18. EVERYTHING HAS MEANING

If you want to convey to your grandkids what you think is important to make a better society, remember that the world around you is the best possible canvas on which to illustrate your points.

- A dripping sink can trigger a conversation on how water actually gets to us and the role of conservation in our lives.
- A ceramic owl on a shopping center overhang or the wires blades whirling above an outdoor billboard offer multiple themes: Why some want birds kept away; how animals and humans have to share space; why acts of seeming kindness (spreading bread crumbs) may end up being a disservice.
- A homeless person pushing a shopping cart loaded with possessions should not be ignored. We won't presume on the comment you will make, only that if the time is *not* right for a discussion on the issue of homelessness, tell the grandkids you are hitting the PAUSE button on your brain to be able to talk about this topic at a later time.

19. WHAT'S REALLY IMPORTANT

Like sponges absorbing water, kids can take on only so much new information in a given amount of time before their mental computers overload and they need a rest before processing anything additional.

So think through what is important to you before starting—what societal principles you really want your grandchildren to carry with them into the future. Is it:

- The Golden Rule: Do unto others as you would have them do unto you?
- The idea that action should always wait until the facts are amassed to illuminate a problem and anticipate its solutions?
- Adaptation to public issues of John Wooden's famous dictum to move quickly but never hurry.^
- The lesson that everyone should try to understand a situation but never judge the right or wrong of something he or she has never experienced.

Merely suggestions. Start jotting your own list of principles in the margin now!

20. FOR THE PARENTS—PART A

We adapted this piece from an EMail we received from a friend, who got it from someone else, who passed it to his entire mailing list, and so on. Clearly, it's making the rounds because a lot of people believe in the message being conveyed.

Grandparents, or those of an age to be one, are often criticized for the deficiencies of the modern world. We know we have to take responsibility for all we have done. But, upon reflection, some of us would like to point out that it wasn't the grandparents who took:

- The melody out of music—
- The pride out of appearance—
- The romance out of love—
- The commitment out of marriage—
- The togetherness out of family—
- The religion out of schools—
- The learning out of education—
- The civility out of behavior—
- The refinement out of language—
- The dedication out of employment— or
- The prudence out of spending.

Remember: Inside every grandparent is a younger person wondering what the heck happened!

There is more to this same EMail on the following page.

21. FOR THE PARENTS—PART B

In noting the changes to modern society, the same EMail went on to suggest that some grandparents may have to deal with them as follows:

YES, I'M A GRANDPARENT!
- I'm the life of the party...even if it lasts until 8 p.m.
- I'm very good at opening childproof caps with a hammer.
- I'm usually interested in going home before I get to where I am going.
- I'm smiling all the time because I don't have the faintest idea what you're saying.
- I'm very good at telling stories over and over and over and over...
- I'm not grouchy; I just don't like traffic, waiting, crowds, stupidity.
- I'm sure everything I can't find is in a secure place.
- I'm sure they are making adults much younger these days, and when did kids become policemen?
- I'm a walking storeroom of facts.....I've just lost the key to the door.
- I'm realizing that aging is not for wimps.

I think I am having the time of my life! Now if I could only remember who sent this to me, I would send it on to others! Have I already sent this to you?

The lesson of this EMail has to be that if we all try to make the world a little better place, while accepting our limitations, we may just be able to do it together.

22. FOR THE PARENTS—PART C

Grandparents come in all kinds of ages and condition; for the most part, how they feel and how they move on any given day determine how well they handle their grandparental responsibilities.

Sometimes grandparents have to realize that age takes a toll on their energy and outlook:

- "Old" is when your sweetie says, "Let's go upstairs and make love," and the response is, "Pick one. I can't handle both."
- "Old" is when getting a little action means you don't need fiber.
- "Old" is when getting lucky means you find your car in the parking lot.

Don't be brave. Grandkids can handle the times when their grandparents feel below par or aren't moving very fast; just spending time together may be enough of a societal lesson until the next time.

23. IT'S THE ADRENALINE RUSH

Although we are not qualified to comment too deeply on hormones and neuro transmitters, adrenaline seems to be one of the most powerful forces stimulating the body.

A surge of adrenaline makes people feel good. Besides its free and not fattening. Start the adrenaline pumping in your grandkids—just getting them excited will do the trick—and they will know that they always feel good when they are with you:

- Create prizes for each grandchild to win. The offer of $100,000 at the St. Louis World's Fair launched a furious competition to be the first to fly a plane on a prescribed course; the chance to win a Nobel Prize galvanizes people to find new and doable ways to solve problems.
- Work on a project together—building, cooking, refurbishing—gives a rush when completed, during the process, and after being admired.
- Competition—hide and seek, checkers, jumping, batting a balloon, bouncing a ball—is a major source of adrenaline during the activity and for the "winner."

24. IT'S THEIR TIME

We have a rule. When we are with the grandkids, we try to devote all of our attention and energy to them. That means we consciously give up our interests or concerns for the moment. We try not to plan any other events at the same time or involvements that might distract us. If you are going to watch television, watch something that they can get interested in as well; if you are playing catch with a ball, don't carry on a conversation with someone else at the same time; if you are cooking, make sure to ask for their help and show them not only what you are doing but why.

It seems only fair. If we want our grandkids to help make a better society for us as well as others, then we need to show them what is expected of them—in detail, under all possibile circumstances, and whenever the opportunity arises.

25. EACH ONE, TEACH ONE

Ever hear someone ask a kid, "How was school today?" A quick "Fine" or a simple shrug is the usual response. Lawyers know that the secret to getting the right answer is asking the right question.

Grandparents can learn the same lesson. Rather than generalized questions, ask your grandchildren about very specific things: "What was the most interesting fact you learned today?" or "What is one thing you heard today that surprised you?" You will be pleased how articulate the grandchildren become in telling you and how easily it starts a conversation that can lead to a discussion of societal values.

One more point: In the 1940s, the Mexican government launched a major campaign to eradicate adult illiteracy. The program urged those who could read to teach someone who couldn't. It was an enormous success. It tells me that we can learn massive amounts of new things from our grandchildren if we always challenge them to teach *us*!

26. RELAX!

One of the most successful books we have written deals with how to organize and manage a party, function, or meeting. It is called *The Essential Event Planning Kit.* It notes the following:

*Creating a major event is fairly easy; it only **seems** more daunting than it actually is. There are three cardinal **RULES** to follow in creating a successful event:*

1. ***Relax!** Don't try to* think *of everything that needs to be done at once. It is virtually impossible.*
2. ***Relax!** Don't try to* remember *everything that needs attention. Jot notes as thoughts come to you.*
3. ***Relax!** Don't try to* accomplish *everything yourself. Let others help by doing tasks for you.*

The same basic rule applies to the responsibilities of grandparenting:

- **Relax!** You cannot single-handledly *re-make* a community. It takes the help of many others and it takes time.
- **Relax!** Your grandkids won't accept everything you say when you say it. Just as Mark Twain noted how much his father had learned during the time Twain was between 12 and 21, so it may take a while for your grandkids to understand your point of view.

SPECIAL TYPES OF GRANDPARENTING

SPECIAL TYPES OF GRANDPARENTING

Nuclear Grandparents

Our focus to this point has been on the responsibilities of *nuclear* grandparents. These are the individuals whose sons and daughters—by birth, by adoption, or as a result of remarriage—are raising their own families.

My wife and I qualify as nuclear grandparents—both her children and my children now have children of their own. But we have no children together. As a result, we are both step-grandparents to the other's biological grandchildren—two of some 90 million Americans (!) who are part of a step-family. For us, the step relationship has no influence on our role as grandparents. Our grandkids are equal. While neither of us has an adopted child—or kids who have themselves adopted—we doubt that our relationship with *their* children would be any different from what we experience with our biological grandchildren.

In grandparenting, *environmental* influences, rather than genetic material, seem to be the dominant force in providing perspective on societal matters. Those who become grandparents to the children of gay or lesbian couples should experience no difference in the resulting relationships.^

When grandparents of a nuclear family are separated from their grandchildren—as we are from two of ours by a distance of 450 miles—we think it actually makes no difference in terms of our responsibilities. We still have the task of telling them our beliefs about important societal issues.

We try to do it when we are with them and through phone calls and mail in between. We send articles, pictures, books, games—anything that makes a point we can reinforce later. We don't do as good a job of this as we would like—to our sincere regret. But we are at least conscious of needing to do better. Since we believe that dealing with societal values knows no age barriers—in fact can become richer as the grandchildren grow older and articulate their own independent views of how society should work—we hope that we will get it right eventually.

Non-Grandparents

We are realize that other older citizens in our society are either not yet grandparents or may never achieve that status for one reason or another. A pity because of the near-universal belief that grandchildren are capable of bringing great joy and blessings to their closest relatives as well as others around them. But just because a person of an appropriate age does not actually have grandchildren at any given time does not, in our opinion, disqualify them from trying to meet at least some of the responsibilities of grandparenting as we see them.

For one thing, older citizens who are not grandparents have as much right as anyone else to enjoy the full benefits of a society—unfettered by anything that might upset them, including the behavior of someone else's bratty grandchildren. As a result, we believe that these older citizens ought to exercise some grandparenting responsibilities toward grandnephews and grandnieces, toward the kids of their godchildren, toward cousins two generations younger, and toward the grandchildren of friends and neighbors.

The concept is the same. Even though a person is not a grandparent, he or she is entitled to live in a peaceful and pleasant community. Everyone living in that society learns at some point that behavior depends on the situation in which individuals find themselves. If a kid is behaving inappropriately in public given the circumstances or situation of the moment, then an older person *ought* to say something to make his or her own situation more comfortable. If done with sensitivity, thought, and care—through parents, friends, or directly to the children themselves—everyone will be better off.

Special Grandparents

But there are also many grandparents among us who fulfill quite different roles for their grandchildren and must meet additional responsibilities to those discussed in this book. We refer to these individuals as *special* grandparents to differentiate them from grandparents who are part of a nuclear family.

Some special grandparents are serving as a substitute parent, replacing a child and/or his or her spouse (perhaps forever) because of divorce, drugs, military or diplomatic service, protracted illness, disability, incarceration, or death. As we think of the energy, time, and sacrifice required of grandparents serving in the role of a surrogate father or mother, we can only appreciate the effort involved. As one expert notes, "Kids often don't act out with [a] parent because they're afraid that will push [them] away. They know the grandparent [acting as substitute parent] is not going to be pushed away. That's why they're an easy target." This book cannot offer any advice to those grandparents serving as surrogate parents; others much more qualified than we are have studied the matter closely and have written on the topic extensively. The fact that these grandparents are unable to concentrate on social values with the same intensity as nuclear grandparents is, of course, understandable.

Cultural Gulfs

There is another group of grandparents who have a difficult time fulfilling the responsibilities that we have outlined here. These are the grandparents who are separated from their grandchildren by the chasm of different cultures. While distance can play a part in cultural differences, it is the dissimilarities between cultures themselves that are far more difficult to bridge.

This situation involves a grandparent who is part of one culture having to relate to grandchildren growing up in a different culture. Take our own case. My wife's four grandparents, although living as adults in the United States, were raised in several different countries; my own four grandparents lived almost all of their lives in countries other than the United States. If that situation were to arise today, what community values should we expect these grandparents to promote to their grandchildren in America?

We have good friends in England who have grandchildren living near them in London and another far away in Los Angeles. When they impart societal values to the grandchild living in the United States, would they be different from those being imparted to the grandkids in England? At first, we thought that they could be. After all, behavior and attitudes acceptable in London are quite different from behavior and attitudes in West Los Angeles, where many English live. How about the differences between Seoul, Korea, and the Little Korea section of Los Angeles?

On the surface they would seem enormous. But since the purpose of imparting community values is to make the *grandparents* more comfortable when they are communicating with or around their grandkids—whether in the United States or in the grandparents' home country—we decided that, whether hard or not, it didn't matter. The only thing that does matter is that the differences are explained and understood. Most kids want to please the people who love them. As a result, we do not think it is hard or difficult to expect kids to adhere to significantly different cultural patterns depending on the situation they find themselves in. Once they understand what is expected in terms of the rituals, habits, patterns, and behaviors observed in different places, you will be surprised at how amazingly adaptive they are.

While some *behavior* in the old country might not be appropriate in the country of the grandkids, it also turns out that many societal values have near universal acceptance. People everywhere want and appreciate privacy, respect, courtesy, and integrity; by the same token, these same people abhor dishonesty, disloyalty, and rudeness. While there are differences in what is considered good manners or dishonesty in different cultures, it doesn't hurt to import the nuances involved into the grandkid's culture. It can make this country a far-better and more interesting place.

Famous Relationships

A few thoughts now on famous grandparent/ grandchild pairings. From our standpoint, they are examples of how some grandparents have met their societal responsibilities to grandchildren.

For more than 100 years, Nobel Prizes have been an important indicator of the progress made in such fields as chemistry, medicine, physics, economics, and literature. There have been nearly a dozen Nobel Prizes awarded *within* families—famously, Madame Curie and her daughter Irene separately for chemistry; Niels Bohr and his son Aage Bohr separately for physics; and husband/wife and uncle/nephew combinations. But there has yet to be a grandparent/grandchild pairing. We have to think, however, that it is only a matter of time before such a combination is recorded.

Some well-known grandparent/grandchildren pairs that come to mind include the Bachs of Germany. Christoph Bach, the grandfather, earned a reputation as a musician. His son, Johann Bach, played the organ, violin, trumpet, and kettledrum in the town of Eisenach—a feat of versatility never seen before. But it was Johann's son, Johann Sebastian Bach, whose work made the family's musical talents legendary.

A more modern version of the grandfather to son to grandson connection in the arts is that of Academy Award-winning actor Kirk Douglas. He appears in the film *Family Jewels* with his son Michael and his grandsons Cameron and Dylan

Douglas. If nothing else, bringing a grandchild into the same profession as that of a grandparent makes the problem of passing a grandparent's values to a grandchild that much easier.

Other occupational pairings of a grandparent with a grandchild include Frank Lloyd Wright, famous for developing the organic style of architecture in the 1930s. Frank's grandson, Eric Lloyd Wright, was an apprentice at Taliesin where Frank taught and worked. Later Eric joined his father, Lloyd Wright, before opening an architectural practice of his own in Malibu, California. Eric notes that his grandfather always insisted that if you want "to learn how to design a kitchen, you have to work in a kitchen." Henry Ford, Edson Ford, Henry Ford II, and William Clay (Bill) Ford, Jr., the Ford Motor Company's current chairman, represent an impressive line of managers who have run the company and developed its business philosophy.

In politics, the Winston Churchill grandfather/ grandson pair come to mind. The younger Churchill, a journalist as well as politician, has noted, "My grandfather's life is a constant reproach to [all of us when we realize] how little [we are] able to achieve by comparison! Not only did he produce some 50 volumes of history, biography, and speeches, but nearly 500 canvases as an artist, some of them of remarkable quality. And in his spare time he managed to beat the daylights out of Adolph Hitler as well." In U. S. politics, two of the better known grandfather/father/grandson connections are Governor Prescott Bush, President George Herbert Walker Bush, and President George W. Bush as well as President William Howard Taft, Senator Robert Taft, and the current governor of Ohio, Bob Taft.^

In sports, the Shea family of the United States provides a poignant grandfather-to-grandson story. Jack Shea won a gold medal in speed skating in the 1932 Winter Olympic Games; his son Jimmy, Sr. was a cross-country skier in the 1964 Olympics; Jack, at the age of 91, was preparing to watch grandson Jimmy, Jr. compete in a sledding sport called skeleton in the 2002 Olympics. Jimmy had been inspired by his grandfather and said that "the best moment was going to be seeing my grandfather in the stands..." Jack never made it. Just two weeks short of leaving for Salt Lake City, a drunk driver killed him. Jimmy, Jr., carried a prayer card from his grandfather's funeral in his helmet when he won the gold medal, saying, "[D]arn it, he's coming with me."

Great-Grandparents

Rather than a rare status as in years gone by, great-grandparents have become an increasingly active presence in the lives of many families. In fact, demographers report that 80 year olds and up are among the fastest-growing segments of the American population. Great-grandparents, too, have a right to a peaceful and pleasant life in the community; age or declining health does not disqualify them. Indeed, their status in the United States has been reinforced by numerous laws, among them the Social Security Act, establishing a health care system for those over 65 (Medicare), and the Americans with Disabilities Act, ensuring equal access to facilities for those in wheelchairs and with other physical handicaps.

In short, citizens beyond a biblical three score and ten are still active and productive; their standards and values are equal in importance to those of younger generations. Having noted all of this and believing that great-grandparents will continue to be an increasing force in the lives of everyone else in society, what role ought they play toward their great-grandchildren? Again, we believe that the role demands more than posing for family pictures, more than expressing admiration over the newest generation in the family. We recognize that when older people become great-grandparents, they lack the energy they had when they first became parents and perhaps some of the enthusiasm when they first became grandparents. But if we don't use the wisdom, experience, and interests their generation developed, we lose an enormously potent and valuable resource to our civilization.

We believe that great-grandparents have specific responsibilities toward their great-grandchildren. But they are different from those they had toward their children or grandchildren. Their children are now grandparents and should assume the responsibilities advocated here for this office within a family; their grandchildren, little babies learning to walk and talk just a moment ago, now have the awesome responsibilities of parenthood. As a result, great-grandparents have to shift to a new role and accept a new set of responsibilities, consistent with their energy, their resources, and to some extent their location with respect to a potentially large brood of great-grandchildren. Specifically, we suggest the following:

Great-grandparents should become the transmitters of family history. Each time

they are in touch with their great-grandchildren, they need to have a little private time when they can tell them a story from the family's past.

Remember, we see the responsibilities of great-grandparenting in the same light as those of grandparenting: It is not something someone volunteers for; it is not a status to be applied for. It comes with the territory of having had children in the first place. So telling a story out of the family's past is, in our view, a solemn responsibility. As such, it takes some thought, some planning, some rehearsal. You want the great-grandkids to get something out of the story, you want them to remember what you tell them. Their attention span is commensurate with their age and stature: short. Because of this, you need to make your stories interesting, fun, brief, and re-tellable by them to their parents and grandparents.

Remember one other thing. The parents of these kids (your grandchildren) will likely relate stories to their children about when *they* were young. By the same token, your children (the new grandparents) may tell their grandkids about their own memories of youth. As a result, we hope the stories told by great-grandparents relate to *prior* generations.

If you are a great-grandparent reading this, suppress your fond thoughts about raising your own children and your adventures with your grandchildren. You have a new job. You have to recapture stories you heard about *your* parents and grandparents. You have to be the linkage between the past and the future. Tell the great-grandkids where your family came from, where they lived, where they went to school, what they learned, what they did to earn allowances, what they achieved, what hardships they endured, what made them proud, what made them sad, how their lives were altered by man and nature over the years.

It is not easy. Make notes. Some of the details may be fuzzy, some you may never have known. Jog your memory with old photos, letters, addresses, documents that you or someone else in the family may have; review a book in your possession or at the library dealing with the time, places, and events impacting the lives of your parents and grandparents. Fill in what you don't know about the family with what you *think* could have been the historical circumstances in which your parents, grandparents, or great-grandparents actually lived.

It probably sounds like a lot of work. It isn't, but perhaps more than most people want. Having said this, will the family even make time for this? Will people sit still long enough to hear anything a great-grandparent has to say? We think so. But even if just one member of the family pays attention, it will have been worthwhile.

When the senior sergeant of a platoon is forced by an officer's death into command in the middle of a battle, his soldiers look to him to take charge, give directions, get everyone out alive. So, too, with great-grandparents. You may not want to be the family historian, but you now have the job. The great-grandkids will love it, the grandchildren will be very proud of you, and your own kids will be happy that you are involved in the larger family. Most importantly, society itself will be better off because you chose to be part of its institutional memory.

So for those who want to participate in this exercise, here is a hint at how to get started. Line up cards or sheets of paper and head each one with a theme or idea for a story. Before long, your thoughts are flowing and your stories will begin taking shape. And society will be better off because of the effort you made.

FINAL THOUGHTS

FINAL THOUGHTS

If someone were to ask you to name the five wealthiest people in the world or to list five of the last 10 World Series or Superbowl winners, it is probable that you would fall short. The remarkable thing is that few of us remember the headlines or events that seemed to demand so much of our energy and attention such a short time ago. We have a hard time even recalling some of the most basic details. It is something we all come to realize: Applause dies; awards tarnish; achievements are forgotten; accolades and certificates get buried.

Some things, though, do not seem to go missing. Take the following quiz and see how you do:

1. List the two most important teachers who helped you on your journey through school.
2. Name a close friend who saw you through a difficult time.
3. Name three people from whom you have learned something worthwhile.

4. List five people who over the years have made you feel appreciated and special.
5. Think of the three people you most enjoy spending time with.

Here is the first lesson from this quiz. The people who make a difference in the lives of others aren't the ones who have the most fame, most credentials, most money, or most awards. They're the ones who care the most about others.

Here is the second lesson. All grandparents should want to qualify in as many of these five categories as possible in the eyes of their grandchildren. In short, ask yourself what you can still do or do in the future to be considered one of your grandchild's most important instructors, meaningful supporters, and enjoyable companions.

Recent events in the Middle East bring all of these possibilities to mind. On a spring evening, a young man entered a mall a few miles from Tel Aviv, paused a moment to watch some children playing, and then made his way to the front of the ice cream parlor where he detonated the explosives packed around his body. The Palestinian man died instantly, as did a 56-year-old Israeli grandmother and her 18-month-old granddaughter.

Of all the images of the current cycle of the Intifada that began with the Passover explosion at Netanya in March 2002, this one seems most poignant. It didn't take the most lives or harm the most people, but the terrible decision of Jihad Titi robbed Israeli society of one of those vital connections between Generations 1 and 3. It prevented one little girl, Sinai Keinan, from making a future contribution toward a better society and it stopped her grandmother, Ruth Peled, from helping to shape the girl's contribution through a sharing of her societal values.^

One of the lessons drawn from the continuing terrorist attacks in Israel and the events of September 11, 2001, in the United States is that most of us are not in control of our destinies. As a result, never assume that there will always be time to impart values to your grandchildren. Give them the benefit of your wisdom whenever an appropriate moment arises and wherever you happen to be.

We recognize that still other circumstances prevent some grandparents from achieving *any* connection to their grandchildren. Divorce seems to be one of the most prevalent causes of this phenomenon. The custodial parent wants to enforce a complete break with the former spouse and/or members of his or her family. We recently learned of another sad example of this phenomenon from a friend. She told us that her own *daughter* has insisted on keeping her separated from her granddaughter for years, refusing phone calls, returning mail and packages to sender, twice calling police during unannounced visits to the daughter's house.

It is often hard for outsiders to understand the forces that can generate such hatred. While both sides in these family wars usually feel totally justified in their positions and believe the other side unreasonable or untrustworthy, we worry about the resulting loss to the *community* arising from such disputes. From our perspective, the social values important to the grandparents cannot be transmitted to the grandchildren in these situations and rather than have a continuation of values from generation to generation, another unguided kid may be loosed on society to ignore accepted standards of civility, taste, respect and other important attributes of a pleasant society.

When we began thinking about the themes for this project several years ago, we assumed that grandparents took their rightful place in society as part of a natural progression. Once people had reached adulthood, they would more than likely have children who would in turn have children of their own.

It now turns out that this type of natural progression does not hold any *legal* status. The California Supreme Court recently held that neither marriage nor biology necessarily determines fatherhood. In deciding that society's highest duty is to look after the best interests of a child, the court held that individuals "can through their conduct become parents." By the same token, the Iowa Supreme Court struck down a state law that gave grandparents the right to spend time with their grandchildren, ruling that it interfered with parental rights. The court put it rather bluntly: "[the statute substitutes] sentimentality for constitutionality."

It appears, then, that genes do not confer any rights or provide any status to those who pass them on to new generations of relatives. In short, grandparents have to do it—in the words of Smith Barney—"the old fashioned way"; they have to earn their place with their grandchildren. We don't see this as a contradiction to anything we are advocating here. Grandparenting, as we see the task, is not the familial equivalent of speed bumps on a street—passive controls that slow speeders without the need for human intervention. Showing grandchildren a way to act and react to different situations in the public arena is a hands-on undertaking requiring grandparents to devote time and energy to the task. As neither age nor retirement gets a person a free ride in terms of jury duty, voting, or helping in a civil emergency, so they should not allow grandparents to escape their responsibilities to the community to help civilize their grandchildren.

An additional thought: If grandparenting has the kind of responsibility that we believe it does it deserves greater respect in the general society. No one needs us to point out that grandparents have jobs, play, love, and contribute as with any other segment of the population. But while popular culture celebrates such television programs about family life as *Father Knows Best, All in the Family, The Cosby Show,* and the *Osbournes,* there is no comparable program looking at the lives, concerns, problems, and duties of *grandparents.* Yes, oldsters have been celebrated in such films as *On Golden Pond* and *Dirty Old Men* and on television in *The Golden Girls,* but these projects involved stories about aging, not the specific role of grandparents in the lives of their communities.

We think the reason for this may be that grandparents are perceived by most to be without interest other than to dote on their grandchildren, without a defined mission toward those grandchildren, and without an important role to play in the society as a whole.

We hope this book will contribute something to disabusing people of this notion. Grandparents do indeed have a substantive contribution to make to the great issues of our time as they impact our individual communities. We hope they will continue to make it as forcefully as they can in the years to come.

APPENDIX

ACKNOWLEDGMENTS

While this book was crafted by me alone, its eventual construction was dependent on the thoughts, opinions, and contributions of others assimilated along the way. My wife, Barbara DeKovner-Mayer (Harris), discussed many of the ideas in the book with me as we have experienced grandparenthood together. She does not, of course, agree with everything I have expressed; and my occasional use of the imperial "we" (as in "we think..." or "we believe...") does not necessarily imply that her thoughts or beliefs are encompassed in that statement. Her real contribution has been in just being there to react to any new ideas I developed. She has forced me to articulate them more sharply until they stand on their own or have to be scratched as too weak to be worthy of inclusion.

In watching my mother, Victoria Harris, deal in her own way with my own three children when they were young and growing—and now reacting to *their* children in her ever-expanding role as a great-grandmother—I realize now that I was observing and absorbing some of her and my father's attitudes toward the duties and responsibilities of grandparenting. Special thanks have to go to my son, Kennith L Harris. He is a wonderful parent, a respected teacher, and a shrewd observer of contemporary social patterns. In discussing the ideas for this book, he was the one who provided me with a professional label for the ideas I was expressing. In short, I came to the concept of situational behavior through him. He also kindly served as one of a panel of readers.

During the course of preparing the book, I had the assistance of some professional researchers in finding some of the material that I quote and some of the examples I use. Special appreciation for their conscientious help goes to Lynn Ecklund and Amy Allen.

I wish also to thank Bill Butler, Bill Gumbiner, David Harris, Michael Harris, and Barbara Linden for agreeing to read the manuscript in its final stages. I have taken whatever comments they made into account in this edition. But please note that they bear no responsibility for the final product and certainly can't be blamed for any errors of omission or commission.

Charles (Chuck) Goldman, as always, provided balanced professional editorial advice and assistance. His careful explanations of grammatical points and his willingness to accept some of my idiosyncratic style habits make it a pleasure to work with him.

Finally, I am indebted to Penny Morensen of The Americas Group for seeing to many of the administrative details inherent in publishing and distributing a book.

BIBLIOGRAPHICAL NOTES

The page numbers in the left-hand column identifies the place where a reference or the first words of a quotation can be found in the text of the book.

12   Many psychologists believe that the personalities, attitudes, and habits of children are nearly totally formed by age 6. As a result, grandparents should not wait until the grandchildren are older and more likely to be with them on their own to fulfill their responsibilities.

"That's it! I'm..." was pictured on a T-shirt in a Paragon Gifts catalog in 2001 and "What I like..." is the caption of a cartoon appearing in the May 19, 2002 issue of *Parade* magazine.

14   "The difference between...," *Los Angeles Times,* June 9, 2002

^   See www.cyberparent.com for a website devoted to parenting. The site also has pages especially for grandparents—articles, discussion groups, tips, and even a discipline primer.

15   For whatever it's worth, 25 percent of all infants cry more than three hours a day. Dr. Harvey Karp, a pediatrician, has discovered a way to replicate the sounds, feelings, and movement of the womb after birth. His ideas are found in a book, *The Happiest Baby on the Block: The New Way to Calm Crying and Help Your Baby Sleep Longer* and were reported in "The Baby Tamer," *People* magazine, June 24, 2002.

16   Raising children is not easy. Programs designed "to rescue out-of-control teenagers through rigid structure, intensive counseling, peer support and strenuous outdoor activities...[are] part of an...industry that has surged in the last 10 years to satisfy...a booming market in parental desperation." While the camps and special schools are praised, "their emergence...reflects the failures...of permissive, distracted parents." As one said: "I don't think there's one of us who has a kid in a program who doesn't feel like we've failed. We're the boomers. We read all the books. We were supposed to raise...perfect kids." Sara Rimer, "Parents of Troubled Youths Are Seeking Help at Any Cost," *The New York Times*, September 10, 2001.

22   A photo in the *Los Angeles Times* (April 7, 2002) illustrates what having fun with grandkids looks like. The picture shows a 4 or 5 year old furiously pedalling his toy car in a determined effort to beat his grandfather's electric scooter in a race down a driveway.

^^   The need to learn how to act in public situations was strongly reinforced in a review of the book, *Esther's Children.* "Jews have lived in Iran for 1,300 years [and] were forced [into] specific neighborhoods...forbidden to leave their ghettos on rainy days (for fear that the rain might wash the impurity off their bodies and onto

Muslim soil) [or]...touch any food or item that may be consumed by a Muslim... [The Jewish] community survived...by preserving their unique identity without ever challenging the treatment they were subjected to. They learned to be vigilant, invisible, and silent."

23 The 2000 U.S. census estimates that 2.35 million American grandparents are permanetly caring for some 5.6 million grandchildren, numbers that have increased some 76 percent since 1970. The Director of Grandparents as Parents, one of some 750 support groups, calls it an "epidemic." The AARP's Grandparent Information Center notes that the phenomenon crosses all socio-economic groups. See "Second Time Around," *People* magazine, September 3, 2001.

30 Situational dress codes are in force everywhere. The authors of a Zagat Guide to Los Angeles Nightlife offer the following advice on gaining admission to restricted-entry clubs: "Arrive well-groomed and well-assembled;" understand that a Prada suit at one place might attract dirty looks at a biker spot next door. "[U]nless you're in a bar with peanut shells on the floor and a game on the big screen...flip flops, shorts, baseball caps or T-shirts will [only] get you...a raised eyebrow from the bouncer." *Los Angeles Times,* June 27, 2002.

31 "to break bad news..." Malcolm Gladwell, *The Tipping Point,* Little, Brown and Company, 2000, pp. 10-11. "If I'm playing...," *Sports Illustrated,* July 1, 2002.

32 In an article on branding cattle—something animal rights groups are trying to abolish—grandfather Larry Buell puts "aside the all-terrain vehicles and...spreadsheets...genetic charts and...online market updates" to take his daughter and *her* daughter out on horseback to rope a calf and burn the family's brand into its hide: "It's our heritage," says Buell's daughter. "This keeps Ashly [Buell's granddaughter] in touch with the way things were." Because what people value about their culture is different, a curator at the National Cowboy and Western Heritage Museum says: "It's easy to say...'it's inhumane' when you're sipping wine in Los Angeles—and your 18 year old has tattoos all up and down his arm and a nose ring too."

36 Speaking of British royalty, Prince Charles spoke of his grandmother and what *she* meant to British society after her death in April 2002. He called the widow of King George VI and the mother of Queen Elizabeth II "a presence in the nation...indomitable, able to span the generations, wise...[a person who served] with panache, style and unswerving dignity...she saw the funny side of life...[with a] wonderful wisdom born of so much experience and...innate sensitivity to life." Audrey Woods, "Prince Charles Remembers the Queen," *Associated Press,* April 1, 2002. If any of us who are grandparents can merit similar words from our own grandchildren after passing on, we will have met our responsibilities.

129

38 See Susan Goodman, "Judith Martin," *Modern Maturity,* March-April 1996. In echo of Martin's words about modern parenting, note the following comments on the $90 billion Tween (7 to 12 year old) market: "More families have two working parents and more discretionary income. And with families under increasing stress...parents have a greater need to believe their children are competent and able to make their own decisions." As an investment banker says: "There have never been so many influences on [these kids], whether it's MTV or the Internet or wealthier parents willing to spoil [them]. [Allowing them to spend money] is a way...to show love to their kids." *Los Angeles Times,* June 27, 2002. A letter to the *Times* on July 1, 2002 noted, "it takes a village [of manufactuers, retailers, media, and other permissive parents] to turn a little girl into a sex object."

39 "Someone once asked..." From an undated page of an issue of *The Wall Street Journal* with a handwritten notation of 1984.

40 "[T]he perfect balance...," *Los Angeles Times*, June 15, 2002.

47 "One of the greatest threats...," Foreword to *Charter Education Handbook*, Character Press, 2002. See also Dr. Marvin Marshal, *Discipline Without Stress*, 2001.

48 "The average age...," Partnership for a Drug-Free America, "The Power of Grandpa," *The New York Times*, September 4, 2001.

50 The idea of rounding up the "usual suspects" to determine whom to blame for lax moral attitudes—when the actual guilty parties are known—is borrowed from the final scene of the movie, *Casablanca.*

51 "In this role...", Gail Sheehy, "It's About Pure Love," *Parade* magazine, May 12, 2002

54 How today's kids successfully manipulate their parents was revealed in a 2002 study of Americans between the ages of 12 and 17 by the Center for a New American Dream. It found that even when their parents say "NO" to a request, six out of 10 keep nagging—an average of nine times—and that 55 percent said their parents usually give in to their repeated requests, particularly about items seen in advertisements. The editors of the *Los Angeles Times* commented on the study on June 30th by noting that the kids learned their nagging skills from parents who "tell 13 year olds to clean...their room nine times [because]...they aren't even listening until the third time [and] don't argue until 6 or 7."

83 The two mottos cited were favorites of Los Angeles banker and philanthropist George Louis Graziadio, Jr., for whom the Pepperdine University School of Management is named. See *Los Angeles Times*, June 11, 2002.

86 Although not independently verified, the story of the standard railroad gauge in the United States made the EMail rounds, seems plausible, and most of all reinforces the point being made.

GRANDPARENTING

89   The discussion of bird behavior and DNA derived from "Birds Do It," an article appearing in the *Los Angeles Times*, June 2, 2002.

91   "A few years ago...," Godfrey Harris, *Don't Take Our Word For It,* The Americas Group, 1998, pp. 87 and 101

93   The dictum is now the title of a 2002 Simon & Shuster book by Andy Hill with John Wooden called, *Be Quick—But Don't Hurry.*

100   "Creating a major...", Godfrey Harris, *The Essential Event Planning Kit,* The Americas Group, Third Edition, 2002, p. 8.

103   Looked at as *organizational* entities, American families are autocratic, loosely federated, independent units run by a collegial decision-making mechanism called parents. Parents decide matters for the indentured members of the unit (basically those under the age of 18) while the freely associated members of the unit (those over 18) accept or reject parental decisions by themselves. The *governance* of extended families involves the coalescence of independent units and/or individuals around particular issues until a satisfactory number or singularly powerful individual unit decides on a course of action.

105   "Kids often don't...," "Second Time Around,' *People* magazine, September 3, 2001, p. 74.

106   The quote, "Kids often don't..." is from *People* magazine referenced at p. 23 above. For more information on grandparents as surrogate parents, see Arthur Kornhaber, M.D., *The Grandparents Guide,* 2002.

109   Data on Nobel prize pairings taken from Baruch A. Shalev, *100 Years of Nobel Prizes*, The Americas Group, 2002.

111   Information on the Bach, Taft, and Ford families is from Internet research; the Douglas family data were found in *Hello!* magazine for April 23, 2002. "the best moment..." and the rest of the story of the Shea family are taken from "A Dream Denied," *People* magazine, February 22, 2002.

120   The events in Israel were taken from articles in the *Los Angeles Times* for May 28, May 29, and June 20, 2002, and *The New York Times* for June 25, 2002.

122   It should be noted that when grandparents serve as the *parents* of their grandchildren, legal guardianship is recommended if for no other reason than to make sure they can make the necessary medical decisions. See reference at p. 23 above. The decision in the California Supreme Court Case, *In re Nicholas S100490,* was announced on June 6, 2002. "[the statute substitutes] sentimentality...," *Los Angeles Times,* September 7, 2001.

INDEX

GRANDPARENTING

GRANDPARENTING

135

ABOUT THE AUTHOR

 **GODFREY HARRIS** has been a public policy consultant based in Los Angeles, California, since 1968. He began consulting after serving as a university lecturer, a U.S. Army intelligence officer, a U.S. foreign service officer with the Department of State, an organizational specialist in President Lyndon Johnson's Executive Office, and as a program manager for an international financial company in Geneva.

As President of Harris/Ragan ManagementGroup since 1968, Harris has focused the firm's activities on projects that offer alternative solutions to matters of community concern. In fulfilling that role, he has specialized in political and economic analysis; marketing public and private sector services through word of mouth advertising; developing new environmental and commercial products; creating commemorative events; and promoting international tourism to various destinations.

Harris has taught political science and comparative government at UCLA and Rutgers University; conducted tourism seminars at the University of Hawaii, Clemson University, and for the US Embassy, London; and lectured on marketing for the Tyrol Tourist Authority, the San Diego County Parks and Recreation Department, and the National Energy Management Institute. This is the 30th book he has written on his own or with associates. He holds degrees from Stanford University and the University of California, Los Angeles.